Building Classroom Communities

Strategies for Developing a Culture of Caring

David A. Levine

Solution Tree | Press

a division of
Solution Tree

555 North Morton Street
Bloomington, IN 47404
800.733.6786 (toll free) / 812.336.7700
FAX: 812.336.7790

email: info@solution-tree.com
solution-tree.com

Printed in the United States of America

FSC

Mixed Sources

Product group from well-managed
forests and other controlled sources

Cert no. SW-COC-002283
www.fsc.org
© 1996 Forest Stewardship Council

ISBN 978-1-935249-91-7

Dedication

THIS BOOK IS LOVINGLY DEDICATED to the memory of my uncle Gabriel ("Gabby") Spector, who will always reside in the community of my heart. I also dedicate this book to the memory of Dr. Arnold P. Goldstein. Much of what I have offered regarding the teaching of social skills and empathy was greatly influenced by Dr. Goldstein's work. I was lucky enough to meet Dr. Goldstein and to be the beneficiary of his encouragement. I will always feel a deep gratitude towards him, and know that his work will continue to touch many.

Acknowledgments

TO MY WIFE, JODI, FOR HER ENCOURAGEMENT and belief in me and for her intuitive insights about education and community. To my son, Samuel, for inspiring me through the revisions with his smiles and cooing as he crawled around on the floor of my office, pulling down books from their shelves. To Bob Barrette, for taking me under his wing when I was a young, wide-eyed teacher and for sharing so many of his creative visions. To Jerry Kreitzer, for his friendship, late-night listening, and his inspiring collaboration. To Lee Domann, for his wonderfully touching song "Howard Gray" and for the friendship. To my parents, who taught me from an early age about community through family and music. To Suzanne Kraszewski, Amanda Samulak, and Jeff Jones at Solution Tree (formerly National Educational Service), for being so wonderful to work with. To my editor, Julia Copeland, whose suggestions I value highly. And to all of the wonderful students and their teachers I have been honored to work with over the past 18 years.

Table of Contents

Introduction: The Beginnings of a Belief System 1

Section One: The Classroom Community 5

Establishing the Classroom Community 5

    What Is a Classroom Community? 5

Transforming a Group of Students Into a Classroom Community . . . 7

    Rituals and Routines. 10

    Common Language, Unity, and the Classroom Culture 12

Making the Case for Community Building 14

Managing the Classroom Community. 18

    Unearthing the Causes of Behaviors 18

    Risk Factors Predictive of Problem Behaviors 19

Nurturing Resilience Within the Classroom Community 23

    Managing Life's Challenges 25

    Self-Perception and Memorable Experiences. 26

    The Quality World 30

    The Four A's of Learning 31

    Two-Person Jobs. 35

The Reclaiming Environment. 37

    Naming the World 39

Section Two: A Culture of Caring 43

Recognizing What We Have Built 43

The Culture of Caring Approach 44

Recognizing What We Must Build On: Social Skills. 45

    The Twelve Essential Culture of Caring Skills 45

Eight Steps to a Culture of Caring 49

1. Name and Model Specific Social Skills 49

2. Be a Listener 53

3. Dialogue With Your Students 56

4. Identify Classroom Goals Together. 63

5. Share Interests and Talents 63

6. Recognize Student Progress and Achievement 68

7. Encourage Your Students' Efforts 70

8. Value Students' Stories. 71

Section Three: Working With Your Classroom Community . . 77

Overtures. 78

Circle of Belonging 78

Web of Life 79

Incorporations. 80

Kitchen Capers 81

Group-Building Exercises 82

Listening and Response 83

Joining a Supportive Environment 85

Team-Building 90

Closure. 94

Section Four:

Teaching Empathy 99

The Birth of a Process 99

Empathy 100

Defining EEA 101

Presenting EEA. 101

EEA Rotation. 104

Role-Plays 104

EEA Journaling 106

Declarations. 106

Rapid EEA Practice: Empathy → Action 108

How to Teach the EEA Approach. 108

Assessing the Need for EEA. 109

Epilogue: Our Collective Purpose 113

Appendix. 115

References 121

The Beginnings of a Belief System

Most people have no time to settle into the essence of a place or the essence of a person and recognize the beauty in that place or person. All living things have it. All living things emanate such grace and beauty, but you don't get energy from it unless you recognize it and honor it. . . . It is not just what you say to the people around you, but what you think.

—Chris Schimmoeller, *A Dance With the Woods* (p. 27)

MY FIRST TEACHING EXPERIENCE was with a fourth-grade class created after the first 6 weeks of a new school year. Two large classes were divided into three manageable ones, and I was hired to teach the new class. The other two fourth-grade teachers chose nine children from each of their classes to go into the new one. You can probably guess what happened. On my first day, I found myself working with 18 young people who were feeling rejected, angry, disappointed, and stupid. I temporarily put my plan book aside and focused my efforts on reconnecting the students to school. Together we sat in a circle and talked about the difficulty of being taken from one class, with all its familiar routines, and being plunked down into a new one. I shared my own misgivings about moving into a new community, teaching in an unfamiliar school, and having my own class for the first time. It was the beginning of an unintentional community-building process. I learned more in that first hour about teaching and making connections than I had in my previous 2 years of graduate school training. Over time we grew into a solid, supportive classroom community where students listened to each other and worked together. Each person felt as if he or she had a place and purpose.

Since that time, as a teacher and then workshop facilitator, I have been in search of ways to replicate what happened spontaneously in my first class. This book is an attempt to share some of what I have found. Teachers, after all, interact daily with young people and can have a profound impact on their lives. The ways in which they communicate with their students, the messages they deliver, and the lessons they teach can help create emotionally coded experiences that make lasting imprints. Such imprints can have a direct effect on a student's self-perception. If the imprint is positive and validating, the emotional memory of the imprinted moment will be positive. If, on the other hand, a child experiences a negative and hurtful event (especially in front of others), that child will feel hurt or scared whenever something happens that is reminiscent of the original event. The child may continue to experience the pain, fear, or anger over and over again long after the original event has passed.

Family counselor John Bradshaw speaks and writes on the impact of parents on children's core beliefs and sense of personal power. He uses the metaphor of a doorknob and its location to illustrate what happens to young people as they deal with the world. He imagines the child in a room with a single door for escape. If the doorknob is located on the outside, the child is not in control over what happens to him or her. If another person wants to turn the doorknob and open the door, it is opened, whether or not the child wants that to happen. Likewise if someone else wants to keep the door closed, it stays closed. The child copes and deals with each situation as best he or she can. However, if the doorknob is located on the inside, the young person can determine if and when the door opens.

When social skills are taught (asking for help, working with others, making friends, making decisions, and solving problems, for example), children have access to the doorknob. The more skills a child has and the more positive experiences or memories that child affiliates with those skills, the more personal power the young person will accrue.

We can help our students develop their personal powers if we work to create a sense of community and connection within the classroom through the teaching of social skills. By consciously teaching social skills and applying them in the classroom setting, the teacher is building a sense of community through shared experience and honorable action. It should particularly be our goal to help produce children who are *resilient*—young people who demonstrate flexibility and adaptability in the face of life's challenges. This book offers guidance in doing just that.

Section 1 deals with the notion of a classroom community and offers suggestions for turning a group of students into a true community of learners. Section 2 spells out the components of what I refer to as a "Culture of Caring." Section 3 provides the practitioner with a variety of group processes and team-building experiences designed to strengthen and maintain the classroom community, while Section 4 focuses entirely on teaching empathy as a social skill in a unit format. Together these four sections will emphasize how to name, teach, and transfer specific social skills while creating an emotionally safe and unified classroom environment.

Section One

The Classroom Community

This is the bright home
in which I live,
this is where
I ask
my friends
to come,
this is where I want
to love all the things
it has taken me so long
to learn to love.

—David Whyte, *The House of Belonging* (p. 6)

ESTABLISHING A CLASSROOM COMMUNITY

What Is a Classroom Community?

A CLASSROOM COMMUNITY IS A PLACE where students feel safe both emotionally and physically, where they feel supported, and where they feel enthusiastic about the discoveries each new school day will bring. It is a place where every individual is honored and where a sense of interdependence is built into the culture. David

Whyte's poem speaks of such a place—where a person feels most at home, free to be his or her own true self without fear of being judged, labeled, or excluded. In this "house of belonging" an individual's unique life experience is embraced, celebrated, and trea-sured; to belong to the group does not mean giving up one's individuality. The classroom community, properly constructed, is also a house of belonging, and students thrive when exposed to the sense of security such a community can provide.

In a classroom community all community members have significant roles to play, just as in a tribal village where each individual's skill and talent is necessary to the survival and function of the group. There is great pride in such a situation; people are honored for who they are, and a sense of belonging and collective purpose is fortified. Malidoma Some (1996) writes:

> Without a community you cannot be yourself. The community is where we draw the strength needed to effect changes inside of us. What one acknowledges in the formation of the community is the possibility of doing together what is impossible to do alone. This means that individual problems quickly become community problems. The individual can finally discover within the community something to relate to, because deep down inside each of us is a craving to be honored and be seen for who we are. . . . In community it is possible to restore a supportive presence for one another. The others in community are the reason that one feels the way one feels. The elder cannot be an elder if there is no community to make him an elder. The young boy cannot feel secure if there is no elder whose silent presence gives him hope in life. The adult cannot be who he is unless there is a strong sense of presence of

the other people around. This interdependency is what I call supportive presence. (p. 25)

It is our challenge as educators to facilitate this "supportive presence" in our classrooms, where kindness, compassion, generosity, and empathy must abound. It is a gift of spirit when a teacher presents numerous opportunities for discovery through inner reflection, outer focus, and direct application. Students not only learn academic, social, and other life skills, but are encouraged to apply those skills by helping, supporting, and honoring others. From this they derive the sense of significance, purpose, and accomplishment that can come from generous community-centered acts. The classroom community is not a program or series of activities but rather a "way of being." It is a belief system that provides the foundation upon which everything that goes on inside our classrooms is situated.

TRANSFORMING A GROUP OF STUDENTS INTO A CLASSROOM COMMUNITY

Michelangelo often spoke of himself as searching to find the figure concealed in the stone, knocking the surface away as if seeking a miner buried in fallen rock.

—Will Durant, *The Story of Civilization* (p. 69)

Forsyth (1983) offers a framework for understanding the development of groups. He identifies five stages, which he calls Forming, Storming, Norming, Performing, and Adjourning (p. 738). These stages are also evident in the process of transforming a student group.

When a group of students comes together as a class (**forming**), the simple model of group development plays out. Sensitively handled, the development can be **transforming**—turning a random group into a true community (and, like Michelangelo, working with the given materials to bring out the positive energy that was already there). The approach is easily remembered as a series of rhyming terms: **norming** *(establishing group operat-* *ing procedures)*, **storming** *(weathering natural dissonances)*, and **performing** *(accomplishing tasks together)*.

In the beginning or formative stage, a group of students and its teacher(s) are not a classroom community but a variety of individuals feeling their collective way through a maze of uncertainties. Guidelines for how the class will operate have yet to be established, and the only social connections that exist among the students are between those who already know each other.

What follows is a process of **norming**. The norms within a class will establish themselves naturally, but it is preferable for the teacher to create them intentionally, working toward the classroom culture he or she desires. If, for example, the teacher encourages, models, and facilitates cooperation, support, honor, and trust as part of the normative process, then the class will begin to internalize those behaviors. If, on the other hand, the teacher says little about the way people treat each other, tolerates subtle forms of teasing, sarcasm, and putdowns (possibly even modeling these behaviors), and speaks to the class in a stern tone from the outset, a far different norm is created—one that may create an atmosphere of fear, a lack of trust, and uncertainty.

In many schools there is often one class that has the reputation of being "the worst class that's ever come through this school." When a reputation of this type is stamped onto a group, it becomes a self-fulfilling prophecy and the norm for that group has unintentionally been established. You might hear students actually saying things like "We're the bad kids" or showing it with their behaviors (with a substitute teacher, for example). Labeling is dangerous: A label can stick, and can be defining. Instead of labeling and mandating, the facilitator of the class- room community must do two things: (1) institute classroom routines and rituals, and (2) establish a common language. These two crucial strategies for classroom community building will be covered later in this section.

Even when norms for cooperation, support, honor, and trust have been created, inevitably, as in most relationships, times of disagreement, conflict, and hurt feelings will emerge. In speaking of classroom communities we refer to this development of conflict as **storming**. Surprisingly, in a well-regulated classroom storms can be useful. When the norms for a class have been specifically named, modeled, practiced, and encouraged, a storm that might ordinarily be destructive can actually be constructive—an opportunity for growth through what Robert Cooper calls "constructive discontent." This term refers to the growth, expansion, and discovery that can come when two or more people are grappling with each other over an issue (Cooper & Sawaf, 1997). The question is, are they grappling *together* to work out a solution to the issue, or are they working *against* each other from two separate and immovable positions? In a healthy classroom community, you are more likely to find people working *together*.

In a classroom community the greater good of the whole is the primary consideration. When individuals see themselves as playing a significant role in the community's healthy functioning, different viewpoints are sought and disagreements are worked out. This opens the students up to the notion of social skills training, conflict management, conflict resolution, and mediation. If these approaches are perceived as relevant by the students, are supported and modeled by the teacher, and interface harmoniously with the norms that have already been established in the classroom and the school, they will prove successful. Otherwise conflict resolution, mediation, or other similar programs will have limited, if any, long-term impact.

A healthy classroom community has taken the time to prepare itself to accomplish its tasks effectively and efficiently without leaving anyone behind and without hurting anyone in the process. When a class understands what the norms are, has been given opportunities to practice and demonstrate them behaviorally, and has learned how to respond to such *storms* as may surface, the class can be said to be **performing** as a classroom community. The time it takes to facilitate the normative stage is a worthwhile investment not only for building a sense of community in the classroom but also in terms of individual and group achievement, classroom management, and emotional stability for the students and the teacher.

Rituals and Routines

A people that lives as a community takes ritual as the soil upon which its future grows. . . . A community that does not have a ritual cannot exist.

—Malidoma Some,
Crossroads: The Quest for Contemporary Rites of Passage
(p. 18)

A ritual is a "regular, consistent practice or activity that sends a clear message—*this is important*"(Greenleaf, 1991, p. 28). Joseph Campbell has written that "a ritual concentrates your mind on what you are doing, introducing you to the meaning of what's going on" (quoted in Osbon, 1991, p. 90). Rituals provide an emotional hook leading to deeper connection to an experience. Think of the sound of the Hammond organ at a baseball game, or the orchestra tuning up before the start of a concert. In each case the ritual prepares the audience for the experience to come.

I worked for a few summers at a youth leadership program called Camp Anytown New Jersey, a diversity program for high school students. Anytown is designed to help student leaders take an active role in their school communities to stop prejudice and bias and to replace these behaviors and mindsets with caring and understanding for all. Each night after a full day of emotional and enlightening shared experiences, the Anytown Community would gather outside our meeting hall beneath the night sky, and sing the song "Freedom" over and over again (*freedom is coming, oh yes I know*). After 5 minutes of singing the entire camp would proceed together down a trail along the lake to what we called the Sacred Fire, where we would end our day with readings, reflections, a song or two, and a goodnight to Anytown. The ritual offered us a way of organizing our responses to the lessons we were learning together. To this day, when I sing the song "Freedom" I remember not just the discoveries we made, but the sense of possibility and excitement that motivated us. That is the power of ritual.

Routines and rituals inherent to the classroom community serve to ground the class in a sense of predictability, belonging, and security. Routines that are intentionally practiced will in time become rituals that collectively serve to create a culture of emotional safety within a classroom (V. Mihic, personal communication, September 10, 2001). A class meeting (see page 59) is a prime example of a ritual. When a teacher begins or ends each day or week, for example, with the students sitting in a circle, taking turns sharing while others listen, asking questions and summarizing for the speaker what is being said and felt, the students know what to expect and come to anticipate a positive experience. A class meeting is the essence of community and social-skill building, for it provides an open forum in which people can share their thoughts, feelings, and ideas knowing that they will not be judged but will instead be listened to and understood. Students will look forward to this daily or weekly ritual of connection, celebration, sharing, and support.

Rituals take many forms. They can be quite simple—writing the daily schedule on the board each morning or playing a few notes on a kalimba (thumb piano) to signify that it is time to move onto the next task or lesson. Rituals help the class flow from moment to moment within each school day while facilitating a sense of self-responsibility along with the sense of safety that comes from a shared predictable experience.

Common Language, Unity, and the Classroom Culture

A common fund of mutually understood words is critical to the functioning of a classroom community. When specific words are connected to the caring vision a class collectively holds, each student in the class can be brought to the same place of focus the moment a certain word is used. This helps to establish boundaries for the group. One word I often use with a class is *focus*. When I say "please focus" the entire group knows that I am asking them to stop talking or working, to look at me, and to listen to my next set of instructions. The words that make up a *common language* help all students start out in the same place in hopes of moving ahead together toward a unified classroom goal.

Common language provides students with something to hang on to as they cross the bridge between their inner worlds (individual thoughts, sensations, and feelings), and the outer world (including the thoughts, feelings, and sensations of others). Students who are taught a concept and given its specific name will more easily internalize the teaching. When we are teaching social skills we can break the ideas down into their simplest components and apply words to those components. Thus all students will know without a doubt what the teacher means when he or she says something like "let's show our *caring* to the new student when she arrives tomorrow."

Often when seeking to collaboratively name a desired behavior with a class, we find that generalities are the norm. For example, *caring* will probably be defined by students as "being nice, being a friend, or helping someone out." My response to answers of this type is that if I close my eyes, I cannot get a clear picture of what is being done. I want the description to be like a script for a play, movie, or television show. So we brainstorm. I divide a sheet of paper into two columns, *looks like* and *sounds like,* and ask the class to fill them in for the term *caring*. From this list we can create a behaviorally oriented definition of caring. We may find that students think *caring* means walking up to a person, shaking his hand, and asking him if he needs any help in his new school (*looks like*), or that *caring* means saying, "Welcome to our school, my name is. . . . Would you like to join us in a game?" (*sounds like*).

When working with students, be sure to provide words or names for as many specific community norms as you can and use these names frequently to reinforce students' understanding of them. In the Appendix you will find a list of 50 specifically named social skills from the book *The Prepare Curriculum*, by Goldstein (1999). All of these terms can, over time, be woven into the vocabulary and thus the fabric of the classroom community.

These first steps, introducing routines and rituals, and creating a common language—are further explained in Figure 1.1 on pages 15–16.

MAKING THE CASE FOR COMMUNITY BUILDING

I often hear the lament, "This stuff is good and I agree with everything you say, but who has the time for these things?" I believe that teachers must make the time, integrating the sense of community and the practice of social-skill building into everything they do. Alfie Kohn, in his book *Beyond Discipline* (1996), wrote the following about a 1994 study conducted by the Child Development Project (CDP) with two dozen elementary schools from around the country:

> Students in the upper grades were asked about the extent to which they experienced their classroom and school as supportive communities. It turned out that the stronger that community feeling was, the more the students reported liking school and the more they saw learning as something valuable in its own right. These students also tended to be more concerned about others and more skilled at resolving conflict than those who

Figure 1.1

Putting Ideas Into Practice:
Norming Procedures for Transforming a Class Into a Classroom Community

1. Use games and exercises to help students feel at ease in the environment.

Several of the exercises detailed in section 3—Web of Life (p. 79), Incorporations (pp. 80–81), and Human Treasure Hunt (p. 94)—are excellent icebreakers that will help students feel at ease.

2. Establish a daily schedule so students know what to expect.

- Post the daily schedule on the board or on a piece of chart paper.

- Be as specific as possible in identifying subjects to be covered, page numbers of books to be read, and any materials needed.

- Set up a morning routine so students know they will

  - Come into the classroom

  - Check out the schedule

  - Get their materials ready

  - Be focused in time for the official beginning of the school day

  - Be ready to help others who may need support

3. Introduce routines and rituals.

- Start each day or week with a class meeting (p. 59).

- Run talking councils, talking circles, or fishbowls any time a pressing issue must be addressed. (See pages 83–84 for an explanation of these activities.)

(continued)

Figure 1.1 (continued)

- Use the Circle of Honor exercise (p. 70) on a weekly basis.

- Have students write journal entries regularly—even daily.

- At the end of each day, award a student who made you smile.

- Introduce focus activities to help tune out distractions and concentrate on the task at hand.

  - **Eyes-closed portraits:** have students, in pairs, take turns closing their eyes and drawing portraits of their partners.

  - **Change-up:** have five students face the class in a row. Move them around while the rest of the class has their eyes closed. When students open their eyes, have them point out who has moved.

  - **Mirroring:** have students, in pairs, face each other and take turns mirroring each other as they slowly make motions with their arms and hands or make silly or serious faces. Have them alternate roles (leader, follower) at the ring of a bell or the clapping of hands.

4. Introduce the rudiments of the common language.

Use the brainstorming columns (looks like; sounds like) to create behavioral guidelines for the following terms:

Caring	Encouraging	Cooperation
Listening	Acceptance	Appreciation
Supporting	Empathy	Courage

---

didn't feel part of a community. What's more, these positive effects were particularly pronounced in schools that had more low-income students. (p. 103)

In other words, the positive effects are more than worth the effort. And not only does community building foster conflict resolution skills, but it is also effective—in fact essential—in heading off potential student violence. John Hoover and Ronald Oliver, in their *Bullying Prevention Handbook* (1996), state that the most significant aspect of anti-bullying or violence prevention initiatives is "the notion of community." They claim that without a sense of cohesion and mutuality, "all efforts to reduce violence will be, at best, stop-gap measures" (p. 93).

The positive effects of community building reach beyond the classroom and beyond the schoolyard. Henry T. Stein and Martha E. Edwards (1998), describing Alfred Adler's concept of *Gemein-schaftsgefühl,* or *feeling of community,* explain that the Austrian psychiatrist believed that

> if people have developed social interest at the affective level, they are likely to feel a deep belonging to the human race and, as a result, are able to empathize with their fellow humans. . . . [A]t its heart, the concept of feeling of community encompasses individuals' full development of their capacities, a process that is both personally fulfilling and results in people who have something worthwhile to contribute to one another. At the same time, the concept denotes a recognition and acceptance of the interconnectedness of all people. (p. 67–68)

Community building, and participation in a classroom community, should be seen not as some kind of activity or lesson but as a *way of being* that touches all aspects of the school day—in the classroom, at lunch, on the playground, going to and from school—and carries over into the rest of life. This way of being creates the conditions to meet the most profound emotional need any person has: the need to belong. When a sense of belonging exists within the classroom, student motivation will be high, performance will be enhanced, relationships will grow stronger, and the classroom atmosphere will be joyful and supportive. These dividends are great returns on the investment it takes to build community. Though community building is not an easy task in terms of time and energy, it is nevertheless a worthy one, considering the multitude of needs shown by students who walk through our classroom doors each morning.

MANAGING THE CLASSROOM COMMUNITY

Setting up the classroom community is just the beginning. Once this collective success has been achieved, the serious work of managing the community, and thus influencing student behavior in positive and lasting ways, can be undertaken. Very often the young people we work with bring behavioral problems into the classroom. Dealing with these behaviors is essential if the community is to function in a healthy way. Luckily, the community setup is ideal for the work of influencing, and when necessary modifying, behavior.

Unearthing the Causes of Behaviors

Each day, as we work with children, we are met with a variety of behaviors, attitudes, and moods. How we respond to these dynamics, which are individual to each child, is critical not only to our students' daily lives but to our own as well. When we are faced with difficult or undesirable behaviors, we need to work to understand them. Every behavior has an underlying cause. If we seek to stop or punish the behavior or order a child to change an attitude, we are not addressing the cause, and most likely our orders and threats of punishment will have a short-term effect at best.

A primary prevention and early intervention approach for addressing any type of problematic behavior is to unearth the cause or feeling and to then seek ways to address that cause. The pressures in a child's life are coming from all directions. These pressures reveal themselves in a variety of ways. For some children it might be a question of whether or not they remembered their house key when they left for school in the morning. For others it might have been the dilemma of what to wear to school. For still others it might be not having understood the previous evening's homework assignment and the fear of what might occur when they arrive in school without having completed it. Some problems may be part of patterns begun in the earliest years of life, in which weak attachment to a primary caregiver shows up as antisocial behavior triggered by a seemingly unrelated or insignificant event. No matter what causes the pressures, the feelings are real and often overwhelming. What we encounter is the behavior, which is the manifestation of the pressurized feelings many of our students live with each day.

Risk Factors Predictive of Problem Behaviors

Researchers David Hawkins and Richard Catalano (1998) have identified risk factors that predispose adolescents to develop problem behaviors. Many of these behaviors, such as substance abuse, delinquency, teenage pregnancy, dropping out of school, and violence, are an outgrowth of the inability to manage the pressures that arise from difficult life situations. These difficult life situations provide an important guide to where to focus our efforts when seeking to build a classroom community when working with children of all ages, not only adolescents.

According to Hawkins and Catalano, risk factors for adolescent problem behaviors are as follows:

Family

- Family history of the problem behavior
- Family management problems
- Family conflict
- Parental attitudes favorable toward, and parental involvement in, the problem behavior

School

- Early and persistent antisocial behavior
- Academic failure in elementary school
- Lack of commitment to school

Individual/Peer

- Alienation and rebelliousness
- Friends who engage in the problem behavior
- Favorable attitudes toward the problem behavior
- Early initiation of the problem behavior
- Constitutional factors

To effectively decode a student's behaviors it is important first to understand how easily and unintentionally an adult can trigger in a student negative feelings about his abilities in school or his relations with adults and other students. This usually happens when that adult himself is provoked by the behavior of the younger person. If, for example, a student feels unsuccessful and stupid because she doesn't understand an assignment, she may not ask for help. Instead her feelings may lead her to throw her book on the floor, saying something like, "This is stupid," or "I hate this class." This is a key moment of opportunity for the teacher—an opportunity to avoid reacting in a judgmental and accusatory manner, which would only reinforce the student's feeling that school is not a safe place and that adults are out to get her.

Instead of reacting in such a way as to escalate the situation, a teacher must model the same understanding and compassion he or she would expect to see in students, and should respond by seeking to understand what thoughts and feelings caused the behavior. This is done through the application of high-level listening responses. A teacher may ask, for example, "Help me understand what's happening. You seem frustrated. What can I do to help you?" or "When you want to talk about it I'm ready to listen." Compare these responses to the following reactions: "Pick up your book now! Do you want to go to the principal's office? Look at me when I talk to you! Do you act this way at home?" These negative reactions have predictable outcomes: alienation, anger, fear, and loss of trust. Such reactions also create a climate of fear within the classroom for those students who merely witness such an interaction.

This high-level communication approach is useful in all situations with students in the classroom setting. There will inevitably be times of anger, frustration, fear, and embarrassment for some students. If the teacher responds reflectively and without being judgmental, the bonding to the classroom community will be strengthened as a trusting relationship is built. Figure 1.2 outlines strategies for recognizing risk factors and responding communally.

Figure 1.2

Putting Ideas Into Practice: Recognizing Risk Factors and Responding Communally

Strength Bombardment

Suppose you have a child in your class who has an extremely negative self-perception. What would you do? Here is a lesson for use in a community setting:

Have students form two equal lines facing each other, leaving an aisle between them to allow a person to walk through. Have the student you are concerned about walk down the aisle thus formed. As that person passes through, students on either side of the line whisper positive and specific feedback to that person: *You're a great friend. You care so much about others. You are good at figuring out math problems.*

After the student has come through the line, ask what he or she is thinking and feeling. Close the exercise by asking the student to share one hope he or she has for the future.

Comfort and Caring

Suppose you have another student who is angry because a parent has let him down and whose home life is impacting his studies. This exercise helps create a sense of bonding to peers and school.

In this exercise students have the opportunity to learn more about others in the class through sharing of significant life experiences. Students may share positive life experiences as well as negative ones. Students who wish to share may sign up, contracting for up to 5 minutes to share with the group. The rest of the class listens without interrupting as each student talks about some important happening in his or her life. Listening group members may ask open-ended questions, summarize, or reflect the feelings of the person who was sharing.

Close by asking all class members to share one-word descriptions of how they feel at the end of the activity.

NURTURING RESILIENCE WITHIN THE CLASSROOM COMMUNITY

In a study covering almost 30 years, child psychologist and human development professor Emmy E. Werner and clinical psychologist Ruth S. Smith tracked the lives of 698 children on the Hawaiian island of Kauai. The primary purpose of their study was to trace the long-term effects of negative early-life experiences on these children. Drs. Werner and Smith and their colleagues took special note of the children who, in spite of exposure to a multitude of family risk factors (an alcoholic parent, an ill parent, or an impoverished home life, for example), went on to develop healthy personalities, stable careers, and strong interpersonal relationships. They called these successful people *resilient*, meaning that despite the presence of multiple risk factors at an early age, they were able to demonstrate the attributes of a person with "self-righting tendencies" with the capacity to spring back, rebound, successfully adapt in the face of adversity, and develop social competence despite exposure to severe stress (Werner, 1989; Werner & Smith, 1992). In their study, Drs. Werner and Smith sought to identify the protective factors that contributed to the resilience of these children. Protective factors are "individual or environmental safeguards that enhance a youngster's ability to resist stressful life events and promote adaptation and competence leading towards future success in life" (Garmezy, 1983, as cited in Bogenschneider, Small, & Riley, 1991, p. 2).

In Werner and Smith's book *Overcoming the Odds* (1992), they report the findings of their study and the "relationship across time between individual dispositions and sources of support that contributed to resiliency and/or recovery among the high risk children and youths in this cohort" (p. 173). A summary of these school "protective factors" follows:

- Social skills

- Positive peer relationships

- Problem-solving skills

- A sense of independence

- A sense of purpose

- Participation and involvement

- School success

- A caring teacher

- Exposure to models and mentors

- An encouraging school environment that enhances a child's competencies and belief in self

The previous list of protective factors looks remarkably like a list of characteristics of, or outcomes fostered by, the classroom community. Those very protective factors that encourage resilience are part of the everyday workings of the successful classroom community. We can actually, as teachers, exhibit a protective factors mindset. The way we speak, the tone of voice we use, our facial expressions, and the intent of the messages we deliver can be calibrated to reassure students. I often remind myself as I'm working with a student that a particular moment could be one that resides forever in the mind and heart of this child—that I should be watchful. A classroom community is all about creating protective relationships. It is a setting in which all students feel safe and where learning, not fear, is the focus.

Managing Life's Challenges

Many resilient adults point to one specific positive adult they remember from childhood. This person believed in them and made them feel special, cared for, and safe, while teaching them the skills needed to manage the pressures each day could potentially bring. It is important to use the term *manage* rather than *cope* when speaking of facing challenges, because there is a conceptual difference between the two. *Managing* has more of a skills focus—it is active. *Coping*, on the other hand, is passive—one simply deals with the situation. That is why we speak of stress *management*, and why administrators are called upon to *manage* the workings of a school. If I walked down the street and fell into a hole, my merely staying there, living there, could constitute *coping*. *Managing*, however, would involve getting myself *out* of the hole. I could do this more easily if I had the skills to manage the situation, perhaps by calling out for someone to help me. The ability to ask for help is a *social skill* or *life skill*. Many young people and adults are unable to ask for help because they have been trained to see asking for help as a sign of weakness. As teachers, we have the opportunity to teach the necessary social skills to help our students manage the challenging life situations they will surely face. Facilitator and workshop leader Jim Lew refers to the collection of social skills acquired throughout a person's life as the "survival file." ⊕ Classroom experiences

Generally speaking, the survival file consists of practical life skills that a person will need throughout life, such as how to work with and get along with others, how to express feelings in a healthy way, how to respond to rejection and teasing, and how to choose and make friends. Any cooperative activity, group dialogue, or lesson in the vocabulary of feeling will help to fill the

"I can't."

survival file. Figure 1.3 outlines how you can help students create their survival files.

Self-Perception and Memorable Experiences

Parents and teachers these days are often very concerned about the question of self-esteem. Self-esteem is a cumulative phenomenon. It is a perception of self that is built upon a series of experiences, positive or negative. Self-perception, then, is what the facilitator of the classroom community needs to focus on. The problem, of course, is with negative experiences in a person's past. If negative experiences are repeated as patterns in a person's life, they come to be seen as the truth—the way things are supposed to be. Once a negative perception is established it is difficult to change the perception. Educator and author Thomas Turney asserts in his Consistence of Perception Theory that "what we already believe about ourselves deters the acceptance of new beliefs that appear to contradict our existing image"(Turney, 1994, p. 34). Whenever I ask people to think of vivid elementary school experiences from their own childhoods, the first thought that comes to mind is often a negative memory—being singled out for singing out of tune or being told "you're not as good as your sister."

Robert Cooper and Ayman Sawaf note in their book *Executive EQ* that the "brain's reticular activating system (RAS) has been primed throughout evolution to amplify negative presumptions and minimize the positive"(Cooper & Sawaf, 1997, p. 59). Presumably this was useful in the wild, when sorting out dangerous sights and sounds, but now this natural amplification of the negative can become a problem. No wonder certain hurtful experiences are so memorable—they're supposed to be. We are

Figure 1.3

Putting Ideas Into Practice: Helping Students Create a Survival File

Have students write survival skill instructions on colored index cards and laminate the cards. Encourage them to keep these in their pockets or taped to their desks. Here are just a few suggested survival topics:

Setting Goals

Questions to ask myself:

- What is my goal?
- Am I reaching it?
- If not, what is getting in my way?
- What do I need to do differently?
- Who do I need help or support from?
- How will I know when I've reached my goal?

Joining In

Questions to ask myself:

- Is this something I want to do?
- Will I disrupt things if I join in now?
- What is the best way to join in?
  - Ask if I can join?
  - Start a conversation?
  - Introduce myself?
- When is the best time to join in?
  - When they are taking a break?
  - At the beginning of the activity?

(continued)

Figure 1.3 (continued)

Communicating Feelings

When communicating one's feelings, it is important to keep in mind not only how those feelings are delivered, but how they are received as well. There are essentially two approaches when communicating a message to another: a "you message" and an "I message." A "you message" is often accusatory, as in *you made me angry* and can put someone into a defensive posture. An "I message" does not blame or judge, but rather expresses a specific feeling and reason for that feeling, as in *I feel angry when you tease me because I don't like to be teased by my friends.* Teach the students the difference between a "you message" and an "I message." Then have them write the following on a survival file card:

I feel (share a feeling word) _____ when you _____ (describe the behavior of the other person) because _____ (describe the effect the other person's behavior is having on you).

Students can punch a hole in the corner of each index card and use a ring to keep them together. Have them continually write out flash cards for new social skills.

Variation: Students might also keep the social skills listed on the inside of a file folder, adding to the list with each new social skill. This folder can be a physical form of the survival file.

Adapted from Goldstein (1999) and Turney (1994).

---

particularly sensitive, it seems, to having our competency challenged in front of others. Remember when teachers would hand back the math tests in order, from highest score to lowest? Many of those who scored low experienced this as a form of ridicule.

Repeated exposure to ridicule is discouraging and often translates into avoidance and distaste. You might hear someone claim to hate math when in fact what he means it that he hates the *experiences* he had with math.

The opposite of ridicule or embarrassment in front of one's peers is positive recognition. When someone's competency with a skill is recognized in front of others, the accompanying feelings of elation and pride are what Abraham Maslow would call a "peak experience." One peak experience sets up in a person the desire for more (Maslow, 1993). The greater the number of successful experiences a person has, the greater the chance that person will believe in his or her ability to achieve. Thus we see the flow of events from self-competence to self-esteem as continuous and self-reinforcing. In our class we would discuss what it feels like not to understand a lesson or new skill. Then we would focus on how it feels to suddenly "get it." This is sometimes called an "ah-ha" or "satori" experience (the essence of what a peak experience is all about). We had a chart on the wall asking, "Have you had a peak experience today?" Students would write their names and what they had discovered or experienced. At some point during the day we would take the time to acknowledge what the student had done, thus celebrating the individual achievement.

It is critical in a classroom community to surround each young person with a ring of positive experiences, to give those experiences names, to identify the social skills or competencies associated with them, and to replicate this process whenever possible. Many schools have implemented some form of a "catch someone being good" program, which focuses on positive behaviors as opposed to negative ones. This is a positive initiative, and is strengthened when the "something good" is named for the student and reinforced as a competency.

The Quality World

Dr. William Glasser, in his book *The Quality School* (1990), writes: "Beginning shortly after birth, we learn to remember all that we do, or all that happens to us, that feels good. We then collect these very pleasurable memories into what is best called the quality world, and this memory world becomes the most important part of our lives" (pp. 58–59). When a teacher can enter into a space of recognition and support with a student—facilitating inspiration and motivation—he or she has entered into that person's quality world.

Schrumpf, Crawford, and Chu (1991, p. 6) extend Glasser's work by pointing out that when a student is in conflict, the question to ask is "What is the unmet need?" The emotional needs Glasser identifies are as follows:

- Belonging (loving, sharing, cooperating, and being accepted)

- Personal power (achieving, accomplishing, recognition, being respected, and feeling competent)

- Personal freedom (making choices, being given responsibility, and feeling a sense of independence)

- Fun (laughing, playing, and engaging in healthy relationships)

Quite naturally, a person's behaviors or choices are driven by the need to have his or her emotional needs met. As teachers, our first question must be, "How can I best meet this person's needs?" rather than "How can I get this student to stop what he is doing?" Every person has a point of connection that taps into his or her individual quality world. If the teacher can find this place in the student, the chances for establishing rapport are greatly increased. Jason Holder, in his book *Adventurelore: Adventure-Based Counseling for Individuals and Groups* (1999), shares case studies in which he is shown to have been able to establish rapport by finding a pathway into the child's world through physical challenges and their accompanying peak experiences. Once a connection is established, a teacher and student can move together into a trusting relationship. When the teacher discovers what a student's unmet needs are and seeks to meet those needs, the student will have access to his or her *quality world*. Figure 1.4 on pages 32–33 shows activities you can use to help your students access their quality worlds.

The Four A's of Learning

Learning something new in the presence of one's peers can be a great stressor. Everyone knows how embarrassing it can be to give the wrong answer in class. Gerald Edwards (1990) helps demystify the learning process for us by charting "The Four A's of Learning" (p. 12). The first "A," he explains, represents the *Awareness Stage*. A learner becomes aware of *what* the new task is: driving a car with standard shift, for example. When learning how to drive a standard shift, at first all you know is that you're going to drive the car by using a clutch and stick shift. You might feel excited, enthusiastic, and maybe a little nervous.

In the *Awkward Stage* (the second "A"), a learner goes from the *what* to the *how*. Now you are sitting in the car as your teacher describes the task. "Push the clutch in but don't ride it,

Figure 1.4

Putting Ideas Into Practice:
Self-Perception in a Quality World

The following are a few activities you can use to help students access their quality worlds:

1. **Appreciation cards:** These appreciative notes can be given out to students to thank them for particular things they have done or to recognize a specific gift a student has demonstrated, such as helping another student with homework.

2. **Face for the Day:** Smiley face cards or stickers can be given at the end of the day to the student who made you smile. State the specific action that caused the smile. I once had a sixth grader who kept all his smiley faces on the wall of his bedroom.

3. **Student of the Week:** All students get the chance to be student of the week, being recognized not so much for what they do but for who they are. You can put up their photos, with an autobiography, and offer them the Circle of Honor activity (see page 70) at the end of the week.

4. **Teaching at Home:** Assign students the task of teaching one of your class lessons to someone at home. Give them a worksheet to use or have them make their own. Have them report on how the lesson went. Make sure you inform the family that you might do this from time to time (I once had a parent accuse her child of just trying to get her to do his homework). The student may teach the lesson to anyone, even a friend—but not to one of the family pets.

5. **Ritual Objects:** Have students bring something to school that reflects who they are—something of importance to them. For example, I would bring in a rock from the canyon country in Utah where I had an important experience. As I share about my rock I would share what I did and why it meant so much to me.

(continued)

Figure 1.4 (continued)

The rest of the class is encouraged to use their listening skills to learn more about the object and, therefore, the person who is sharing. This is more than show and tell. It is an opportunity to share something about oneself through the symbolic meaning of the object.

6. **Physical Initiatives***: A physical initiative is a group problem-solving challenge in which everyone must be able to work together in order to accomplish the identified goal. Here are a few favorites:

   - *All Aboard:* Create a small area with masking tape on the floor or use a small board. The group has to get everyone in the space and keep themselves intact for as long as it takes to sing "Row, Row, Row Your Boat."

   - *Human Knot:* Ask a group of about 6 to 12 people to face each other in a tight circle. Each person holds out his right hand and grasps the right hand of someone else as if shaking hands. Each person then extends her left hand and grasps the hand of someone else so that each person is holding hands with two different people. The result should be a confusing configuration of arms and bodies—a human knot. The group must untangle the web of arms into a hand-in-hand circle. People may not let go of hands as they work together as a group to untangle themselves.

   - *Moonball:* This is a free-form version of volleyball, without the net. Using an oversized beachball, instruct the class that they are to keep the ball up as long as possible. Time the group and process after a couple of attempts, asking for strategies to make the effort more successful. You can keep this one going all year as the class continually attempts to better its time.

---

*With all physical initiatives, the learning and true benefit comes from the processing. See pages 58 and 60–61 for more on processing.

put the shifter into first gear, watch your rpms, disengage the clutch, give it a little gas, watch for the other cars. . . ." Suddenly you feel overwhelmed, very nervous, and frustrated as the car bucks up and down with a burning clutch not far behind. What you need at this point from your teacher is patience, a nonjudgmental attitude, nurturance, and support. What you don't need is to be yelled at, called names, or told that you never will be able to learn this task. If someone feels hurt or judged while in the awkward stage (particularly in front of peers), the person will be negatively imprinted with the experience and will likely go into the third "A"—the *Avoidance Stage*.

We tell students about this stage, which is a predictable though not inevitable part of the learning process, so that they understand some of the possible patterns of learning. If a learner enters the Avoidance Stage, she may be prone to saying things like "I don't like standard-shift cars; I hate math; I'm no good at sports; I wish I could sing" or more general things like "This is dumb; This is boring; This is stupid." If you have ever heard anyone make statements like these, you have likely heard someone who has had a negative experience when learning a skill or task. Teachers can unintentionally send students into the Avoidance Stage by responding negatively to learning efforts. If a child encounters negative feedback while learning something, that negativity becomes the child's frame of reference. It is unlikely that the child will then be able to develop confidence and competence in relation to that particular task. Teachers can also help students reverse such damage by being patient and encouraging coaches.

The ideal is to provide support to the learner in the *Awkward Stage*. Support can take the form of acknowledgement, encouragement, and practice, so that the skill in question will over time become second nature. When this happens—when you drive the standard and shift without even thinking about it—you have reached the *Automatic Stage* ("A" number four). In the *Automatic Stage* the skill has become ingrained, as we often find it has when we do division, shoot a basketball, or play the guitar. You can teach the concept of the four A's to help children understand that learning is more than right or wrong, stupid or smart. Learning is a *process* that people experience in different ways.

A friend of mine who teaches special education has been able to help students individualize their own learning experience by having them graph where they are along the continuum of three A's of learning—Awareness Stage, Awkward Stage, and Automatic Stage—when learning something new. By understanding the three A's of learning, students are able to see that it's not about being smart or dumb but about where people are as they learn something. Some speed toward Automatic while others, who need more time and practice, linger in the Awkward Stage.

Two-Person Jobs

H. Stephen Glenn, co-author of *Raising Self-Reliant Children in a Self-Indulgent World* (with J. Nelson, 1989), tells the story of how he and his 6-year-old son worked together welding the tie rod to their tractor. When they were finished, his son said, "Thanks, Dad, for letting me help you fix the tractor." Glenn responded that he could not have completed the task without his son. He needed two people to do the job. After this experience, his son would often present his father with a list of all the two-person jobs that had to be done around their ranch. Stephen Glenn identified two-person jobs for his son and in so doing taught him that "when a job takes two, I am sometimes equal to my father, and that makes me very significant"(pp. 56–59).

When a person has success while working with another, that experience takes on an aura of meaning and purpose. When a teacher intentionally provides opportunities for students to take part in meaningful collaborative activities, such as creating a welcoming celebration for a new student or co-teaching a lesson, trust-building is a natural part of the process. The students also are practicing the crucial life skills of planning, negotiation,

---

Figure 1.5

Putting Ideas Into Practice:
Creating Two-Person Jobs

• Always send students in teams of two for any errand within the school—sending a note to another teacher, bringing something to the office, etc.

• Have two students share the responsibility of handing out or collecting papers.

• Assign two students the task of preparing a lesson or presenting to the class.

• Use the concept of two-person jobs as a way of training students to work in groups. (Before establishing any sort of cooperative learning group, have students work in pairs for a long time, calling this training "Two-Person Job Preparation.")

• Assign classroom buddies. When a student is absent or misses a lesson, the buddy's responsibility is to keep track of what was missed and to teach some of the lesson(s) to the absent buddy. (See pages 88–89 for the "We Missed You" exercise.)

compromise, listening, and responsibility. Identify for yourself two-person jobs within the classroom. Whenever there is a task to be carried out, make it a two-person job and find two students to work on it together. See Figure 1.5 for some ideas for creating two-person jobs.

THE RECLAIMING ENVIRONMENT

I was once conducting a series of social skills sessions with some fifth- and sixth-grade classes in a school district near my home. I had already worked with the students on one occasion earlier in the school year, having them practice speaking and listening with someone they did not know well. Now I was returning for a second visit. The day was running smoothly when, as I walked into the classroom of my third class, one of the students immediately called out, "Oh no, this guy. I hate this guy!" Before I could respond directly to the child, he was sent to the principal's office by the teacher for being "disrespectful and rude." My preference would have been to enter into a dialogue with this student about what he was thinking and feeling. I didn't get the chance to find out because he was gone, punished for his behavior.

Later that day I was walking down the hall when who should come out of the bathroom but the same student who earlier had said he hated me. As we neared each other, he stopped, pulled back, and eyed me with a look of uncertainty. I smiled, walking toward him, and we had a chance to speak about what had happened earlier in the day. He told me that he had felt uncomfortable with the activities I had done earlier in the year, not having understood why we were doing them, and didn't want to feel that way again. I told him I understood and that he could feel free to ask questions in the future if he ever felt uncertain about what we were doing. He liked this idea and immediately agreed. He never resisted again, and in fact became very helpful in the discussions, often asking clarifying questions, and always willingly partnering up during group work.

There is a tendency to judge a person's behavior and to punish that behavior immediately (often in front of others), instead of determining the behavior's cause. If the cause can be identified, the teacher has a place from which to work in seeking to help a student reconnect to his or her environment while learning from his experience.

Brendtro, Brokenleg, and Van Bockern, in their book *Reclaiming Youth at Risk* (2002), write that "to be reclaimed is to be restored to value, to experience attachment, achievement, autonomy, and altruism"(p. 69). A reclaiming classroom environment is one that reconnects the young person to a world of safety and trust, painting a new hopeful picture of what life can and will be by offering new perspectives in familiar places.

In speaking of a "familiar place" I refer to a *habitual survival strategy*—something a child has learned in order to feel emotionally protected. A student who feels nervous, scared, or anxious when learning something new may have figured out that when he talks back in class the teacher will focus on how "bad" he is rather than how "stupid" he is. This talking back, this behavior strategy, is for this student a familiar place.

Once a strategy like this becomes ingrained in the psyche of the child, it becomes a subpersonality and weaves its way into the fabric of that child's relationship to the world, even if that subpersonality or strategy is not always necessary or if it proves, over time, to be self-destructive. The student who acts out in class may continue this behavior into adulthood, becoming unable to sustain trusting working relationships with superiors, possibly having difficulty in keeping a job (Brown, 1983).

Molly Brown, in her book *The Unfolding Self* (1983), refers to these subpersonalities as our "loyal soldiers" because they will battle to the end, loyal to the cause of meeting our emotional needs, protecting our psyches from further emotional trauma. Brown speaks of the Japanese marine who famously, years after the end of World War II, was discovered on an island. "Unaware that the war was over, he had continued to obey his orders" (p. 18). If one's loyal soldiers are allowed to operate as they always have, they become strengthened and more difficult to retrain. Brown continues: "When the initial purpose of a subpersonality is recognized and honored, it is often possible to reclaim the purpose and energy while letting go of the role or form. Other, more appropriate ways of meeting the need can be found. The Japanese marine was brought home from his island and no doubt found a new role for himself in society"(p. 19).

In a reclaiming environment where a student has acted out, a teacher who sees the situation as an opportunity for growth can enter into a dialogue with that student to explore together what the student was feeling, what he could have done differently, and what he can do next time. The teacher can, in other words, retrain one of the student's loyal soldiers. It is not a matter of judging or punishing a behavior but rather of providing a perspective on why the student did what he did. It is necessary to honor the work of the loyal soldier before the retraining or reshaping begins. Figure 1.6 (p. 40) offers some practical strategies on creating helpful dialogues.

Figure 1.6

Putting Ideas Into Practice:
Suggestions for Helpful Dialogues

Explain to students that it takes courage sometimes to step away from what others are doing. Invite them to consider the following topics, collectively exploring the variety of choices available at any moment in one's life, and the potential long-range impact of those choices:

• The need we all have to belong, to be cool, to have friends

• The way many of the choices we make reflect our need to belong

• The effects our choices may have on others as well as on ourselves

• The way things we experience today can become memorable experiences later on in life

• The fact that at this stage in a young person's life, he or she can still make choices that will change his or her future for the better

Naming the World

One teaching strategy for reshaping the environment is known as naming the world. Beginning in the late 1950s, educator and social activist Paulo Freire was working on an adult literacy project among the peasants in his native Brazil. Freire's challenge was to teach these illiterate workers how to read. What Freire soon found was that the ignorance in which these people lived forced them into a "culture of silence." The rulers of the country had power and voice, while these peasants had neither. Freire found fault with the existing system of education, which he felt enforced the social inequities already in place. Instead he developed his own system, a "pedagogy of the oppressed," in which he taught people to appreciate what they already knew, to take control of their own knowledge and to create, with some assistance and encouragement, their own educations. This was achieved through a process Freire called "naming the world," in which dialogue between humans created a shared sense of what the world was—a process of defining the world and the place of the self within that world. Freire's process of learning brought with it a sense of dignity. He not only had success in teaching his students how to read but, more significantly, he helped them come to "a new awareness of self stirred by a new hope." Their newfound awareness gave them more power over the quality of their day-to-day existence (Freire, 1993, pp. 57–71).

From Freire's work and subsequent discoveries regarding the relationship between learning and a person's sense of hope and dignity we can perhaps derive the following lesson: *That which is unnamed is invisible. A teacher's job is to help students name the world.*

Once something is named for a person, that person will have the ability to re-create it, change it, or stay away from it. The things people do well—their competencies—can also be named. Once they have been identified they can be put into the survival file. Unless something is named for us we might not know it exists—we might not be aware of it. This is the great gift a teacher can bestow upon a student: making the invisible visible. John Hoover and Glenn Olsen, in their book *Teasing and Harassment* (2001), utilize what they call the *frames and scripts* model to help children develop a "problem-solving attitude" to help them manage various low-level forms of aggressive behavior. The essence of this approach is to provide a vocabulary for the student along with a script that can be used by the adult who is intervening and by the student with his or her peers. A teacher can thus provide assistance in naming feelings and ideas that might otherwise cause dangerous frustration. A teacher can participate in a dialogue that helps a student *name the world*. Freire says that by naming the world people transform it, and that "dialogue . . . is the way by which they achieve significance as human beings" (p. 69).

Dialogue is the essence of a classroom community. It is through dialogue that teaching occurs. Most of the exercises in this volume are aimed at facilitating various kinds of dialogue. All of the recommendations in the next three sections have to do with using dialogue—the communal naming of the world—to enhance learning.

Section Two

A Culture of Caring

Without reverence, our experiences are brutal and destructive. With reverence, our experiences become compassionate and caring. We shall come to honor all of Life sooner or later. Our choices are when that shall happen, and the quality of experience that we shall have as we learn.

—Gary Zukav, *The Seat of the Soul* (p. 58)

RECOGNIZING WHAT WE HAVE BUILT

ONE YEAR WHILE TEACHING SIXTH GRADE, as I watched my students acting compassionately toward one another while working on a group activity, I found myself thinking, "I wish someone could come in here and see this." It was mid-October and I was excited because it was obvious that my students were practicing the habits I was seeking to promote—the habits that create a culture of caring. A culture of caring is a moment-by-moment practice of compassion for others, embodying a sense of reverence for life. A place where such habits are practiced is a safe space, one in which honor and compassion are the norm and connectedness is the outcome. It is all about the teacher's intentions, about modeling and encouraging and even ritualizing the behavior we call *caring*. When caring is identified and practiced without fail, when it is ritualized, its significance is highlighted and it becomes the cornerstone of the classroom community.

As a teacher, I have always believed that little things are big things. We never know when a moment with a child will be stamped as a lifetime memory. When building a classroom community, it is imperative to intentionally create a ring of safety or protection for our students through the types of lessons we teach, the opportunities for growth we facilitate, and the rituals and responses we model. We must pay attention to the way we speak with one another, the way we work together, and the way we overcome and work out disagreements and challenges, keeping in mind the goal of showing care and compassion for all.

It is with this goal in mind that I present the materials that follow. They include a description of components of a culture of caring, discussion of ways to implement the ideas in your own classroom, and various specific exercises that will help you in your quest to make a culture of caring the prevailing culture within your own classroom.

THE CULTURE OF CARING APPROACH

The Culture of Caring Approach is a classroom-community-building strategy designed to help students achieve academic and social success through the creation of a learning environment that is physically and emotionally safe. The approach is based on the Social Development Strategy developed by David Hawkins and Richard Catalano and used in their *Communities That Care* training program. The Social Development Strategy seeks to encourage healthy behaviors by reducing risk factors and simultaneously increasing protective factors (Hawkins & Catalano, 1988, pp. 13–15).

In the Culture of Caring Approach, when students' physical and emotional needs are met, motivation for achievement and learning new skills will be high. Chief among the effective tools is security—the security provided by routines, rituals, and use of a common language. When the classroom environment is hopeful and resource-oriented—a "reclaiming" environment—students will not only find the opportunity to identify and name social skills and helpful behaviors, but will be able to practice and apply those skills in a setting in which uniqueness, diversity, and individual expression are celebrated. When this happens students feel bonded to their classroom experience and to each other. They enter the "house of belonging."

The suggestions in this book can be applied in almost any order. The key is a teacher's attitude and intent. When we model caring behavior for our students, we will inevitably create a caring environment.

RECOGNIZING WHAT WE MUST BUILD ON: SOCIAL SKILLS

The Twelve Essential Culture of Caring Skills

It's easy to feel instinctively that we know what social skills are and what we must teach our students. After all, we reason, these things are obvious and natural. It can be quite another thing, though, to try to come up with a list of exactly what these behaviors and skills are that we seek to transfer to our students. This is why naming the world is such an important practice in everything we do—it helps us focus as we reach toward our community-building goals. When the Culture of Caring is firmly in place in the classroom, the environment is one that is gentle, focused, challenging and encouraging—much like a loving parent. If you are to prepare students for the future social challenges life will surely hand them, you should focus on certain social skills. There are 12 social skills I most often teach to prepare the students to manage any difficult life situations they will face.

1. **Listening**—Listening is a core skill for truly understanding the needs and feelings of others. Caring will be strong in a group in which listening is important.

2. **Empathy**—Empathy is more than a feeling; it also is a skill of compassion that can be demonstrated. Empathy in practice carries with it a tone of reverence and honor.

3. **Knowing, managing, and expressing feelings**—Students must have their vocabulary for feelings expanded beyond *good, bad, sad, mad, nice, okay,* and *fine* (the words I most often hear). By creating a glossary covering the spectrum of feelings, we are enhancing a young person's means of expression. Expanded expressive ability can help students manage frustration and anger.

4. **Intuitive (inner) listening**—This skill is a version of decision making that comes from trusting oneself to do the right thing. We can teach students that we often instinctively know the best choice in any given moment, that the challenge lies in trusting and acting upon one's thoughts, feelings, and hunches.

5. **Making and keeping friends**—Just because people desire to belong and make friends doesn't mean they know how to do so. This skill requires application of a bundle of

skills: listening, empathy, working with others, keeping one's word, encouraging others, and having a conversation. All of these applied in combination offer a formula for healthy friendships.

6. **Responding to teasing**—A teasee's response to a teaser's overtures can either stop or exacerbate them, leading to higher level aggressive behaviors (taunting, putdowns, bullying), hurt feelings, or worse. Students must be taught how to respond clearly and honestly, saying things like "I don't like it when you say those things to me. I would like you to stop." They must also be taught to distinguish between good-natured joking and hurtful teasing. Hoover and Olsen (2001) use simple visuals in the "frames and scripts approach" to teach these distinctions to young people and allow them to see another's perspective.

7. **Asking for help**—Children and adults alike often avoid asking for help out of fear of appearing foolish or incapable. In a caring classroom, asking for help is an invitation to others to put caring and support into practice. It is crucial to dialogue with your students about the importance of asking for help and to provide them opportunities to do so. If a student asks for help, receives it, and doesn't get teased or made fun of, he will not only have his confusion cleared up but will also discover that asking for help is a healthy and productive skill.

8. **Helping others**—This concept can be presented to your students as a skill. It is an art to offer help in a way that does not invite prideful resistance in another person. A student can be taught caring gestures—lending a pencil

or a book, for example, or offering to study with someone who might be having difficulty in understanding a new lesson or concept.

9. **Working cooperatively with others**—Cooperative grouping is considered a protective-factors strategy because it allows bonding through the application of a variety of social skills. Inevitably though, there will be disagreements. When groups break down, you may find a perfect teachable moment, allowing students to examine what it takes to work with others. You can facilitate a dialogue about how hard it is to work cooperatively, eliciting from students ideas about how to work more effectively as a group.

10. **Solving disagreements with others**—Negotiation and the ability to compromise are key components of this skill. It is natural to have disagreements or conflicts with others. What doesn't often come naturally is the ability to respond in a relaxed way in order to work toward a mutual solution. We can teach mediation skills, helping students learn to hear both sides of any story. A socially competent student is able to listen to the other side of the argument and express his or her viewpoint in hopes of achieving a mutually acceptable resolution.

11. **Greeting**—The ability to look someone in the eye, offer a firm handshake, and say "my name is…, welcome to our classroom," or something else appropriate to the situation, is a crucial life skill and community builder. Often when we train students to be peer mediators we present the greeting as an essential aspect of the session because

it helps people feel comfortable in what is potentially a stressful situation.

 12. **Goal-setting**—The discipline required to declare a goal and follow through on it is important in working on any new caring skill. Also, if the class is encouraged to support others as they work on their individual goals, uniqueness within the group is nurtured as well. Goal-setting should be part of everyday classroom culture.

EIGHT STEPS TO A CULTURE OF CARING

A teacher who wishes to sensitize students to the essence of a classroom community where recognition, honor, and compassion are the norm must model these behaviors. Certainly it is possible to model such behaviors instinctively, without thinking. But it's safer and more efficient to do so with forethought. With this in mind, I offer here eight *culture of caring strategies* a teacher can intentionally model and integrate into the classroom environment.

1. Name and Model Specific Social Skills (12) prior

Name the world of social skills for your students. Fill up their survival files. The goal in teaching a social skill is to allow students to internalize the skill as a thought process they can access automatically to turn into action in the anxiety of the moment when they are in real-life situations (see Fifty Social Skills to Consider on pages 115–116). Arthur L. Costa and Bena Kallick use the term "habits of the mind" when referring to such automatic responses, indicating that the behaviors require a discipline of the mind that is practiced so as to become an ingrained way of working toward more thoughtful, intelligent action (Costa & Kallick, 2000).

Identify the skill (name it). Frame for the students what specific skill they will be experiencing.

Sample scenario: You say, "Who has ever had a disagreement with a friend? Today we will learn what to do if you are having a disagreement with another person."

Brainstorm with the class the types of things students get into disagreements over. Some common responses you most likely will hear relate to the friendship issues of jealousy, loyalty, breaking a promise, and exposing a secret.

Refer to the previously taught skill of listening and how listening helps people understand each other better when they are in conflict. Get them thinking about communication, verbal and nonverbal, and then highlight the importance of listening. Listening is not often thought of as a communication skill, but it is the most important one because it helps us understand other people, lets other people know we care about them, and helps others understand us.

Teach the skill (model it). Role-play the skill with a student volunteer in front of the class and have the students give you feedback on how you did in demonstrating the skill.

Sample scenario: Demonstrating with a student volunteer, ask that person a question. For example: "Why didn't you invite me to go to the movie with you and Raul? I thought we were friends. You're a jerk and I'm mad." Instead of modeling effective open-ended questioning, talk at length about all the annoying things you think this friend has done. When you stop, ask the class for feedback: "How did I do? Was I a good listener? Was I able to find out what happened? Did I give my friend a chance to explain?" Stress that a big part of dealing with disagreements is to get all of the information first, before you do or say anything that might be hurtful.

After the class responds, ask for some specific strategies of the types of questions you might ask. Repeat the exercise with the same student, this time combining feeling statements with open-ended questions ("I was feeling left out when I found out you went to the movies with Raul. Was there a reason you didn't invite me?") As your partner responds, model understanding, showing you can see the other person's position. Ask the class to identify what you did differently. After someone observes that you stated how you felt, asked questions, and then summarized back what the other person was feeling, present the following guidelines for working out disagreements with others:

1. Decide whether or not you and the other person are having a disagreement.

2. Tell the other person how you feel.

3. Ask them what happened.

EXPLICITLY POSTED

4. Listen to what they say.

5. Think about why the other person might be feeling the way they do or why they did what they did.

6. Suggest a compromise or a way to work out the disagreement.

Practice the skill (in pairs). Have students role-play the skill with each other, taking turns. Students who wish may role-play in front of the class.

After presenting the guidelines for working out disagreements with others, pair students up and provide them with a series of scenarios. Have them choose who will be the listener first (the listener will ask questions and provide summary statements).

Sample scenarios:

- Even though you weren't invited to a party your friend was invited to, your friend is still going.
- One of your classmates lost a book you loaned him.
- You and your friend want to do a different activity.
- Your friend told your secret to someone else.
- You feel that your classmate keeps bossing you around during a group project.

Have each pair work through the guideline steps, working out the problem in public, through discussion and compromise. Then reverse roles and have the pairs talk about the same topic once again.

Process with the group. As a large group, share challenges, concerns, insights, and applications.

Process the lesson by asking some or all of the following questions:

- What was difficult for you?
- What was it like to be listened to?
- What did you learn or what surprised you?
- Where could you practice this skill in your own life?

Be sure to teach all skills in the same manner. Chances for success are greatly improved if the following factors are in place:

- There is a safe and supportive classroom setting.
- The learning sessions are specific and focused.
- All students are involved.
- There is relevance to real-life experiences.
- Skills are over-practiced (this helps make the skills automatic).
- Students report to the class or group the day after they use a specific skill.
- Skills are periodically reviewed.

2. Be a Listener

I was once talking to a seventh-grade student about the mediation program in his school when he spontaneously turned to me and said, "I like going to mediation. They always listen to me there." The "they" he was referring to were the mediators, and listening is essentially what they are trained to do. Listening is one of those skills organizational development specialist Robert Cooper has characterized as "common sense but not common practice." Listening is also the first skill listed in the first category in the 12 Essential Culture of Caring Skills. There is a good reason for this. In my informal interviews of teachers during workshops, I have found that when I ask about characteristics of their most memorable teachers, "someone who listened to me" is one of the most common and heartfelt responses. Listening is one of the greatest gifts one person can offer another. Its importance is all the greater when it is offered by an adult to a child—by a teacher, for example, to a student. When a teacher models listening behavior it must be more than mere theatrics—it must be listening with focused intention, taking in the entire thought and responding for understanding. There is no place in this act for defensiveness, anger, or blame. In the book *Kitchen Table Wisdom* (1996), Rachel Naomi Remen writes:

> Perhaps the most important thing we ever give each other is our attention. And especially if it's given from the heart. When people are talking, there's no need to do anything but receive them. Just take them in. Listen to what they're saying. Care about it. Most times caring about it is even more important than understanding it. (p. 143)

Listening is a critical interpersonal skill, and yet it is one of the most elusive. It is not often that people are taught the skill of listening, though it is certainly an expectation that people will listen when someone else is speaking. The question for teachers is how to teach listening so that students will relate to it as a meaningful skill.

Listening is not just a social skill—it is also considered a life skill, in the sense that an effective listener increases his or her potential for future success and happiness at work and in the home. Daniel Goleman, in his work on emotional intelligence, points out that "We're being judged by a new yardstick: not just by how smart we are, or by our training and expertise, but also by how well we handle ourselves and each other. . . . The new rules predict who is most likely to become a star performer and who is most prone to derailing" (1998, p. 3). Listening and empathy are two critical emotional intelligences that help us make healthy connections with the other people in our lives.

Sensing where other people are "coming from" is what listening is all about. Often conflicts between two people stem from the inability of one to understand what the other one needs. We may think or assume we know, but unless we ask, it's only speculation. We must teach young people how to listen as a way of understanding others, helping them make positive connections, and setting the stage for empathy, that centrally important attribute toward which our efforts are leading. (In section 4 you will find empathy presented as more than a feeling—as, in fact, an advanced listening skill that can be learned, practiced, and applied.)

When we interact with another person, the way we respond will affect the quality of the interaction. People often misinterpret telling their own story as listening and connecting. An example would be if you started to tell someone about a challenge you were facing in your classroom and that person interrupted you to tell you about a time when a similar thing happened to him. This is usually followed by advice giving, which Thomas Turney identifies as a low-level listening response. To create an environment in which high-quality listening is the norm, it is imperative for the teacher to model *high-level listening,* or *helping responses* (Turney, 1994, pp. 55–56).

According to Turney, the three highest levels of listening responses are:

1. ***Open-ended questioning.*** Open-ended questioning occurs when the listener asks questions to draw out or invite more information from the speaker. Such questions often begin with *who, what, when, where,* and *how.* (Although *why* can begin an open-ended question, it is a word that will often put a person on the defensive, whether or not that is the

intention.) These questions are intended to communicate interest, curiosity, and support for the person who is speaking. In contrast, closed questions can be answered with either a *yes* or a *no*.

2. ***Clarifying and summarizing.*** Clarifying and summarizing are the listener's way of checking in to make sure that he or she is really understanding what is being said. This takes a great deal of concentration, requiring the listener to be present and focused on the person speaking. Summarizing also helps the speaker keep his or her thoughts and ideas clear and focused.

3. ***Reflecting feelings.*** A listener who is reflecting feelings responds to the combination of tone of voice, nonverbal cues, and the issue itself. This is probably the highest level of listening one can offer. The purpose is to create a caring and nurturing interaction by accurately reflecting the speaker's feelings. This response is perceived by speakers as less intrusive than actual questioning.

Figure 2.1 on page 57 offers practical techniques for practicing listening with students.

3. Dialogue With Your Students

Dialoguing is a group process that emphasizes the all-important skill of listening. It is sometimes referred to as the art of collective thinking. In dialogue we interact verbally (conversing, questioning, responding) with students in positive ways, getting information while exploring issues collectively as a class. During a dialogue session the group explores a topic or concept, trying to increase understanding through questioning and clarifying.

Figure 2.1

Putting Ideas Into Practice: The Listening Wheel

When learning the skill of listening, students benefit from frequent practice. This exercise offers excellent practice techniques.

Instructions: Students form two tight circles with equal numbers in each—an inside circle and an outside circle. People on the inside circle face out, while people on the outside circle face in. Students may stand or sit face-to-face to form pairs. You may give them a set of practice questions to work with (see list below).

The next step is to ask the first question of the people on the inside circle, while the people on the outside circle act as listeners. The job of those on the outer circle is to listen and ask open-ended questions. The inside-circle group must answer the questions. After 2 or 3 minutes, stop the group and reverse roles so that outer-circlers answer and inner-circlers listen.

After each person in both circles has answered the first question, students on the outside circle move two places to the right so they have a new partner. Start the process again with a new question.

Listening Practice Questions
Here are some sample questions and topics to use when practicing listening with your students:

- What is your favorite season?
- Can you tell about a place you would like to visit?
- What is the best book you ever read?
- What is something you feel good about?
- Can you tell about one of your goals?
- Where do you feel most accepted?
- What do you look for in a friend?
- Who is the most important person in your life?
- Whose life have you influenced for the good?
- What do people like best about you?

You can ask questions or present a variety topics of your choosing. The process is listening; the content is up to you.

No one's responses are judged. Responses are just listened to and questioned for understanding if necessary.

In a true classroom dialogue, the teacher isn't the center of attention. In the true spirit of community, the thoughts, feelings, and ideas of everyone in the class are the center of attention. Students are not only allowed to have a voice but are invited to share it. This spirit is nurtured when the teacher is in the habit of asking questions for understanding and summarizing ideas and returning them to the students. The teacher thus acts as a facilitator. Dialogue in the classroom is invitational—this approach creates a setting in which all ideas are welcomed, respected, and understood. For additional information on dialoguing, see Senge, Roberts, and Ross (1994), and Figure 2.2 (p. 59) on conducting a community meeting.

Processing. Processing is a form of dialoguing. The "process" we refer to is that of examining what people are thinking, feeling, or sensing. For example, when used in the classroom, processing may help students identify the reasons for doing certain activities or lessons and to understand what they can potentially learn. There are various ways and times to process. It can be done during a lesson or at the end of a lesson. Processing with a class is important because most of the learning comes out of processing what is happening or what has happened when working together. The skill can eventually be transferred so that students can process for themselves whenever they are working on a task alone or with others. Because processing is a form of dialoguing, and dialoguing is dependent on listening skills, it will come as no surprise to find that open-ended questions are key. Some questions I like to use are these:

Figure 2.2

Putting Ideas Into Practice:
Conducting a Community Meeting

A community or class meeting is an effective way to facilitate a dialogue session. This meeting is an open forum in which your class or group can share thoughts, feelings, or ideas about a relevant topic. The guidelines for a community/class meeting are as follows:

1. Group members sit in a circle. Students speak when they have something to say. It is not necessary for everyone to speak, nor is it necessary to raise your hand.

2. The rules for class meeting are as follows:

   • Speak one at a time.

   • Honor others.

   • Speak for an "I," not a "we."

3. Meetings can serve many purposes. They can

   • Prepare the class for a task at hand (a new lesson, a class project)

   • Allow participants to give and receive feedback about work in progress

   • Allow class members to share concerns about something that has happened

   • Help students review learning

   • Allow students to share positive outcomes from working together

- How are you feeling?
- What are you thinking?
- What did you learn?
- What is one word that describes the group?
- What is one thing that surprised you?
- What one thing do we need to change in order to be successful?

Processing helps everyone understand how the group is feeling and validates concerns some people may be having (especially if others in the group express similar concerns). I once was involved in a physical challenge with my sixth-grade class in which we had to get everyone over a 10-foot wall without any apparatus for assistance. A facilitator guided us, instructing us that we were to use only our bodies and must be considerate of each group member. Immediately two of the strongest boys determined our plan, which involved putting the smallest girl over the wall first. Within 20 minutes we had everyone over and were celebrating our accomplishment. It was at this time that the real learning took place. The facilitator had us sit in a circle and share how we felt about the activity. As we went around the circle rating the experience numerically (1 being the lowest and 10 being the highest), everyone rated it a 9 or 10 except for the girl who had been sent first over the wall. She rated it a 1. The facilitator asked her to explain. She said that she had a fear of heights and that no one had asked her how she felt about the plan. The tone of the group immediately changed. The facilitator looked around the circle and asked, "What is more important, getting over the wall, or *how* you get over the wall?"

This was processing in action. We would not have gotten the same lesson had we ended with our unquestioned celebration of victory. Processing can move us beyond the business as usual, can push us past our easy interpretations of events and into deeper consideration, maybe even reconsideration, of motivation.

The inner voice. Dialogue is not always conducted with others. We have internal dialogues, too. It is unfortunate that use of the inner, or intuitive, voice is not often taught as a social skill, because it can be one of the greatest clarifiers of behavioral choice. So often young people have told me that they knew full well that something they did wasn't the best thing to do and yet they did it anyway. In the end they and others had their feelings hurt, or worse. I have dialogued with students about their inner voice in relation to personal safety as part of abduction prevention education, but it is also easily applied to the workings of a cohesive classroom environment.

The inner voice is essentially an inner guidance or intuition system. Once you have identified and named it for your students you can refer to it when exploring the concept of decision making. Daniel Goleman (1998), writing about the power of intuition, says that "people can sense intuitively in the first seconds of an encounter what basic impression they will have of the other person after 15 minutes—or half a year." He suggests that "such instantaneous intuitive astuteness may be the remnant of an essential early warning system for danger, one that lives on today in feelings such as apprehension" (p. 53). If students can learn first that they *have* an inner voice and second that they can trust what they hear, think, feel, or sense, they can learn to make healthier decisions. Figure 2.3 offers a strategy for teaching students about their inner voice.

Figure 2.3

Putting Ideas Into Practice: Accessing the Inner Voice

I like to begin the lesson with an explanation such as this: Have you ever left home and suddenly realized you've forgotten something such as your homework or lunch? Once you thought, "Oh, I forgot that," you were able to get whatever it was you forgot before you were too far from home. But who said, "Oh, I forgot that"? This was your **inner voice**. The inner voice talks to you with unexpected thoughts or physical feelings and sensations (saying, for example, "this just doesn't feel right").

• Pass out index cards and have students write down one situation in which their inner voice gave them a message.

• Once the cards are completed, have students mingle, holding their cards at chest level for others to see. They are to connect with as many people as possible, quietly reading what they've written before moving on to someone else.

• When you signal, have partners sit down and talk about their direct experience with the inner voice.

• After 15 minutes, run a community meeting in which the inner or intuitive voice is explored in more detail. Invite students to consider how people can learn to better trust their gut responses or hunches.

At this point, students will be curious about the phenomenon known as intuition. This leads to lively conversation about how people often know what the right thing to do is. You can explain that the inner voice also tells you what others in your class need when they are struggling or having a tough day.

4. Identify Classroom Goals Together

classroom contract/chart

It is crucial to establish boundaries as part of establishing the norms of a class. Whenever I visit schools I usually see the rules posted on the walls of the classrooms, in the cafeteria, the hallway, the library, and any other place where students might see them. Often these rules are stated in the negative, as in *Don't put people down*, *Do not call out in class*, and other similar directives. But there is another approach. Instead of telling the students what you *don't* want them to do (the rules), you can create a classroom contract in which their input is requested (see Figure 2.4, pages 64–65). You can ask, for example, *What do you want to get out of this class?* and *What are you willing to give to this class?* We can refer to such paired questions as *gives-to-gets*, accentuating the implied relationship: One gives something to get something. The teacher also offers his or her own gives-to-gets. The contract can be structured around the answers to these gives-to-get questions. A classroom contract helps to establish the norm that everyone in the classroom has a say. Everyone understands that students can monitor and influence each other.

CULTURE OF LEARNING
– Listen
– Care
– treat ppl. well

5. Share Interests and Talents

By sharing your interests and talents, you humanize who you are and strengthen students' sense of connection to you as a person. A classroom environment that promotes community provides a variety of cooperative experiences for its students. Whether it's group initiatives and problem-solving challenges, or listening exercises and simulation games, the goal is to help the students experience the uniqueness and value of each moment shared with others. There are many ways to gain insight from one's life experiences, and you never know when a valuable life

– Be friends w/ everyone

– Share yourself.
– make connections w/ one another.

Figure 2.4

Putting Ideas Into Practice: The Classroom Contract

The classroom contract is a norm-setting procedure between the teacher and students that not only establishes group goals, but also determines each person's responsibility in reaching them. The Classroom Contract also introduces the notion of interdependence and collective purpose while acting as a team-building process. Students write answers in a list without regard to spelling, sentence structure, or grammar. Students need to be concerned only with the ideas.

• Ask students: "What do you want to get out of this class in terms of knowledge, skills, and personal awareness?" Students write answers in a list without regard to spelling, sentence structure, or grammar. Students need to be concerned only with the ideas.

• Once students have completed their lists, have them find partners with whom to share what they have written.

• After 10 minutes, have pairs find two other pairs to form groups of six. Each group creates a synthesis of the ideas, creating a single list.

• Have an already prepared list of what you will offer to the students under three categories: *knowledge, skills,* and *personal awareness.* Show this list to the class at this time and invite each group to compare its list to the teacher's. Each group puts a check next to each item the teacher has listed and circles each item not on the teacher's list.

• The teacher negotiates with the class specific items to be added to the contract and writes these items on a sheet titled "Add-ons."

• After this step, the class is told that the lists they have just created contain what they will get from the school year. Because this is a contract, they are to brainstorm a list of *gives-to-gets* with the teacher. These will be lists of things they are willing to do (what they are willing to give) to get the positives they have

(continued)

Figure 2.4 (continued)

(what they are willing to give) to get the positives they have already listed. After brainstorming, go over each give. Ask for clarification if necessary. Then ask if there are any who can't give something on the list. If someone can't give something it is taken off because this is a group contract and everyone will be held to it.

• The teacher then displays her gives-to-gets to the class, explaining any items if necessary.

• The final step is the teacher's list of non-negotiables—rules everyone must live by. It should contain no more than five items.

Here is a sample contract:

What We Hope to Get

Knowledge and Skills
• Meaningful Lessons
• Fun Activities
• Success and Achievement
• Life Skills

Social/Emotional
• Safe Learning Environment
• Friendship Skills
• Improved Relations With Others
• New Friends

What We Are Willing to Give

Class Gives-to-Gets
• Attention
• Participation
• Respect to Others
• Best Effort
• Nonjudgmental Attitude
• Helpfulness
• Willingness to Do
  Assignments

Teacher Gives-to-Gets
• Work
• Patience
• Feedback
• Knowledge
• Dependable Preparation
• Understanding
• Care
• Nonjudgmental Attitude
• Flexibility

Non-Negotiables
• Follow School Rules
• Avoid Put-Downs

Process developed by Gerald Edwards. Source: Turney, T. (1994). *Peer Leadership: A Human Relations Process to Reduce Substance Abuse and Improve School Climate.* Mountainside, NJ: Turney, pp. 12–13.

lesson will crop up. I have learned that the process of teaching itself can be our greatest advisor, for as we teach, we learn. But we are not the only ones in the classroom who can teach. We learn from our students every day, but we can make the lesson more official if we want to. By providing our students with the opportunity to plan and teach a lesson, we can facilitate the joy and sense of giving that come from teaching and helping others.

Teach the teacher. One year while teaching sixth grade in New Hampshire, I created a month-long unit called Teach the Teacher. I wanted the students to realize they had unique skills and talents that I did not have and that they could teach me how to do many things. Often something a child can do well, such as setting up a tent or making a ceramic pot, is a family activity or interest. One goal with Teach the Teacher was to connect what we were doing in school to the child's life at home. Every Friday four or five students taught me a lesson they had prepared. The rest of the class observed the lesson and offered feedback afterward. I learned many things that year: how to juggle tennis balls, slalom ski (in simulation), how to feed and care for a hamster, and how to make three-dimensional designs.

One day, two students asked if they could teach me how to ride a horse. "You can put the saddle right on that telephone pole lying on the ground," I said as I looked out the window. They both looked up at me, smiling. "No, Mr. Levine," said Ruth Ann, "you don't understand. We want to bring the horse to school. My mother said she would bring the horse to school, and we could teach you on a live horse." The girls did not know of my fear of horses. I told them: "I'm afraid of horses, and I might be too afraid to ride. I'll do my best, but I can't promise anything beyond that." Looking puzzled, Ruth Ann and Reagan slowly walked away.

A couple of weeks went by, and the big day finally arrived. The class was seated in a circle as we waited. Suddenly somebody shouted, "They're here!" With that, the entire class leapt to its feet. "Sit down now!" I said too loudly. "I want your support out there. Whatever you do, do not make a sound. I don't want you scaring that horse!" We all marched outside. The girls had brought a beautiful horse named Donnybrook for me to ride. I was standing about 5 feet away from Donnybrook. That seemed close enough. Ruth Ann said, "Mr. Levine, you can come a little bit closer." I went up, she took hold of my hand, and together we started patting the horse.

For the first 15 minutes, Ruth Ann and Reagan taught me how to groom the horse. I brushed Donnybrook's soft mane and coarse tail. After a few minutes, I was feeling pretty comfortable as I found myself digging dirt out from around the horse's shoes. The girls asked if I was ready to ride. "Yeah, I'm ready," I replied casually, trying to sound relaxed. I must have appeared as frightened as I was because Ruth Ann looked at me and like a teacher to a student said, "Mr. Levine, are you okay?" The tenderness with which she said this and the care in her eyes made my shoulders drop, and I relaxed. I was okay! I got onto the horse. Reagan held the reins and walked us around in figure eights for about 10 minutes. When I got off Donnybrook the class gave me a standing ovation. As I looked back toward the school, I noticed every class on that side of the building watching the lesson from the windows.

The real learning took place after the ride, when we went inside. We sat in a circle and asked the girls questions and commented on the riding lesson. I asked what their reasoning was when they taught me how to groom the horse as the first part of the lesson. I had assumed it was to help me feel more comfortable around Donnybrook. Ruth Ann and Reagan said that yes, they felt that grooming the horse would relax me but, more important, they were covering themselves in case I was too afraid to ride. They reasoned that if I declined to ride, at least they would have taught me something and fulfilled the assignment.

I realized that their critical thinking skills had been put to the test and they had passed magnificently. Their behavior also reinforced my belief that open-ended assignments based on student trust can flower into something far beyond any teacher's expectations. The universal reaction from the class was something like "Mr. Levine, you're always telling us to feel safe in the classroom and to take risks with things we're not really comfortable with. You proved to us you believe that. We knew you were scared, but you did it anyway."

Guidelines for setting up your own Teach the Teacher unit are provided in Figure 2.5 on page 69.

6. Recognize Student Progress and Achievement

The emotional need for self-competence has to continually be fed. One bad day, embarrassing moment, or low test score can tear down a person's positive sense of self. It is critical to be an observer and respond appropriately to the needs of your students while encouraging your students to do the same for each other. There are classroom techniques for practicing this kind of behavior. One I particularly like to use with students is the Circle of Honor, which is explained in detail in Figure 2.6 on page 70.

competition

– Achievement Wall (fluency)
– Group celebrations
team

Figure 2.5

Putting Ideas Into Practice: Teach the Teacher

Teach the Teacher can be a short unit or part of a year-long plan. If you set it up at the start of the school year, every student can have a chance to teach, either as part of a group or as an individual.

Teach the Teacher Sign-up Sheet

Include the following:

• Names of students teaching the lesson
• Topic of lesson
• Materials needed
• Space needed
• Estimated duration of lesson
• Evaluation technique (How will you know I have learned what you are teaching me?)

More Teaching Applications

Brainstorm additional teaching ideas with your class. They may come up with some such as these:

• Allow students to teach the occasional math or language arts lesson.

• Invite school personnel—the principal, other teachers—to watch demonstrations of lessons students have taught the class (how to make origami swans, how to prepare some favorite food).

• During Parent Night, have students set up teaching stations where they can instruct parents, just as they have instructed the teacher and the other students.

• Have students write "life lesson" books that they can share with students in lower grades, reading the book aloud, discussing the lesson, and finally giving the book to the younger child as a gift.

Figure 2.6

Putting Ideas Into Practice: The Circle of Honor

The class sits in a semicircle with the student or students being honored as the focus of the group and seated in a special chair. They are honored by being listened to as they share something of importance to them. This could be something they have written or otherwise created, or some exciting and joyful news. Students can also tell the class about a challenge they currently are facing in their lives, and the class can offer caring suggestions for consideration.

A sample situation that has often come up for me is the student who shares with the class the information that she will be moving after the upcoming vacation. Students will understand how hard it is to move away from a familiar school and friends. They may suggest that she set up an e-mail correspondence with students or make periodic phone calls to check in. The class could make a card to send and people can make plans to visit—all to ease the student's transition to a new place.

This is a ritual for uninterrupted celebration or support. The key skill to practice in the Circle of Honor is the skill of listening. The key emotion is the feeling of connection.

7. Encourage Your Students' Efforts

Encouraging an effort is different from praising an outcome. Encouragement levels the field because all people have the ability to put forth their best effort, and they will if their needs are met and fear of failure in front of others is absent. That's what a classroom community is all about—risk-taking in an atmosphere of safety and respect. When competition with winners and losers among classmates is lessened, honor for individual expression and uniqueness is heightened.

Angeles Arrien (1993) defines honor as the capacity to confer respect on another individual. "We become honorable," she writes, "when our capacities for respect are expressed and strengthened" (p. 15). When students are conscious of the words they use and the support they offer through these words, they are practicing honor language. Students understand that the saying "sticks and stones can break my bones, but names can never hurt me" is untrue. As Robert Fulghum (1988) points out, "words can break your heart" (p. 20). Ask your students what the familiar explanation "I'm only kidding," used after a hurtful remark, really means. Whenever I ask this question I ask if the old sticks and stones saying is really true. Students will say it is *not* true—that names and words do hurt. I write on the board, "Words can become memories." Then when I ask if "I'm only kidding" really means the person is joking, they will respond "No—if it hurts someone's feelings it's not a joke."

Tell them about Dr. Martin Luther King Jr.'s advice: If you're going to say something about someone you should ask yourself three questions—Is it nice? Is it true? Is it necessary? If you can't say "Yes" to all three questions then you shouldn't say anything.

Figure 2.7 on page 72 offers one strategy for integrating the concept of honor language into your classroom.

8. Value Students' Stories   *autobiographical personal interviews*

Inside each of us is a unique expression waiting to find its path into the world. To help young people find that unique pathway and give voice to this part of themselves, we must intentionally seek to find new ways to understand more about them. One way of doing this is to provide students with the opportunity to tell

journaling

Figure 2.7

Putting Ideas Into Practice: Honor Language

Put up a sheet of paper on the wall in your classroom. Title it "Honor Language." Encourage students to write any of the following information whenever an appropriate moment arises:

• The name of a person who has said something honorable to them

• An honorable phrase someone has used

• The name of an honorable person in history

• An honorable act a person did for someone else in the classroom

Periodically invite students to share entries on the sheet and process them with the class.

their stories. So often in schools and communities young people are labeled or judged rather than listened to and understood. A theme throughout this book is the need all people have to belong, to be accepted, and to be a part of the group. To feel separate from people and events is essentially to feel, as Terry Tafoya (1992) has said, "dis-membered," or cut off, from the group. Much better to be *re*-membered, and that's why our stories are so important, for they allow us to share who we truly are.

Stories keep people, memories, and life's lessons alive. The oral tradition of storytelling has been around forever as a way to connect with others while passing down valuable life lessons. Stories provide listeners with new information to add to their unique worldviews. Tafoya talks about the "schema theory," which sees each person's worldview as a set of blueprints that provide a guide for living. People also have the ability to borrow patterns of behavior from other people and from nature, adding these patterns to their schemata, and making them their own.

Tafoya has revealed for me what his Native American culture teaches: There is much to be learned from the world around us, for it reflects back to us what we are supposed to see. If our classrooms are places where people can honor others for who they are by allowing them to tell their stories and by listening to each unique voice, there will be a greater hope for all young people to grow up whole. The word *whole,* meaning *healthy* or *sound,* is related to the word *heal.* To be healed or whole is to be resilient. Emmy Werner's (1989) description of a resilient person as someone who "loves well, works well, and plays well" is what we as significant adults can help create and uncover.

There are many excellent exercises a teacher can use to encourage student storytelling. Of course autobiographical writing and journaling are among the most useful techniques we have open to us. But there are others. One of my favorites to use with a class is the personal interview. It is a community-building exercise that helps students understand each other better while practicing their listening and inquiry skills. Figure 2.8 on page 74 offers further information on conducting personal interviews.

The activities I've included in this section are more than icebreakers or even skill builders. Most significantly, they are processes that will help you inculcate the concept of a Culture of Caring in your students. There are so many hurtful behaviors students have learned somewhere in their lives, usually as a means for emotional survival. The Culture of Caring approach seeks to teach new ways of being with others—ways that promote a sense of connection

Figure 2.8

Putting Ideas Into Practice: Personal Interview

Students should sit in groups of 6 to 10 in a horseshoe configuration. Students can use sheets with interview questions, either those you have given them or those they have brainstormed beforehand. Each student gets a turn sitting in a chair at the opening of the horseshoe while the others interview him or her using the questions on the sheet. After 5 to 10 minutes the student being interviewed thanks the group for listening and asks someone to summarize some of what was said. The person who summarizes then sits in the interview chair. This process continues until all voices have been heard.

Here are some sample interview questions:

1. How many people do you have in your family?

2. What is something you do well?

3. What awards have you received or would like to receive?

4. Tell us about something you feel good about.

5. What is one of your goals in life?

6. What is your favorite thing to do on a Saturday morning?

7. What kind of music do you listen to?

8. What is a challenge you are facing in school?

9. Tell us about a favorite birthday.

10. How would your parent(s) or guardian(s) describe you?

Adapted from Turney, T. (1994). *Peer Leadership: A Human Relations Process to Reduce Substance Abuse and Improve School Climate.* Mountainside, NJ: Turney, p. 64.

and emotional safety. Unless a child feels connected to the school experience and the people he or she encounters there, learning will be compromised as emotional survival becomes the primary focus during the school day. It is my hope that the Eight Steps to a Culture of Caring will provide a specific pathway for you to travel in your quest to build a classroom community.

Section Three

Working With Your Classroom Community

A CLASSROOM COMMUNITY, with its focus on empowering the individual, offers what psychologist Carl Rogers (1980) calls "a person-centered approach"—a group experience in which a participant "can become increasingly autonomous and creative as the architect of his or her own life" (p. 183). In such a classroom young people can learn about themselves and others through a series of connecting experiences. It is a place where support and encouragement reign, where students feel as much joy in being providers of help and generosity as they do in being receivers.

In this section you will find a number of classroom exercises designed to encourage the kind of communal classroom atmosphere most conducive to fostering autonomy in students. This is a section made up entirely of suggestions for putting ideas into practice. These exercises are designed to help students develop the kinds of social skills they need when building not only the classroom community, but other communities throughout their lives. All the exercises are intended to encourage generosity and

empathy in students. All are community-building and commu-
nity-strengthening exercises. The exercises are independent, and
may be used in any order. I have organized them here according
to the part of the learning process—beginning, middle, end—to
which each exercise most lends itself.

OVERTURES

Some of these exercises are particularly well suited for use as
icebreakers, either with a new group of children at the beginning
of a term, or with any class as the first exercise of the day. The
Circle of Belonging is particularly effective as a warm-up routine.

Circle of Belonging

At the beginning of a group or class experience (or outdoors if
you prefer), place a circle of rope on the floor, making the circum-
ference large enough so that everyone can enter comfortably. Tell
the class that inside the circle is the *circle of belonging* where everyone has a place.* Play some music, beat a drum, or clap a rhythm,
and tell students that when they are ready, they may cross over the
rope to enter the circle. When all have entered, stop the music or
drumming and stand together quietly. After a few moments let
everyone know that they are all standing in *the circle of belonging*
and as long as the class is together for the school year, they will
symbolically be standing inside that circle. If a new student comes
into your class, have the students explain the circle of belonging,
spread out the rope, and invite that person in. At the end of the
year, step back inside the circle and have the students step out as
they move on to their next school experience.

---

*This is a variation on a process learned from Bill Plotkin and Dianne
  Timberlake.

Web of Life

Have students sit in a circle, preferably on the floor. Sitting with them, equipped with a roll of string or light rope, share your name and something of interest about yourself, such as: *My name is David and sometimes I play fiddle for square and contra dances.* Holding the end of the string, roll the ball across the circle to another student. That person continues the sharing and then, holding onto his or her end of the string, rolls the ball across the circle to another student. This process continues until everyone has shared some information. By the time the last person in the circle has spoken, the group will have created a connecting web of string. This is a wonderful metaphor for the interdependence that develops within a classroom. Students enjoy this illustration of how everyone is connected in some way, particularly through the sharing of personal information.

I often use this activity as a way to learn the names of the students when I first meet them. It is helpful any time you want to teach a lesson on interdependence and the skills we will need if we are to work together for a successful classroom or learning experience. You can use this process at any time as a unique classroom experience that encourages all to share. An interesting way to close this exercise is to ask the class what should be done with the web of string. Some will suggest putting it down on the floor and leaving it there for a day. Others might suggest diagramming the interconnections. Still others may suggest that the group reverse the process, sharing some new information as the string is wrapped up back into a ball.

Incorporations

The purpose of this activity is to increase the general energy level of the class by getting people to move around, mix, and have fun. The task for the students is to form and re-form groups as quickly as possible according to the teacher's directions. The teacher calls out a description of a kind of group, and the students must respond as quickly as possible by forming groups to match the teacher's descriptions. Once the teacher stops the action (use a slide whistle or something similar), another group is called out. Here is a sequence I use:

- Groups of three

- Groups of three plus one

- Groups of five in which each person in the group must have one item of clothing which is the same color as that of someone else in the group

- Groups in which all members share the last digit of a phone number

- Groups of eight in which members have to arrange themselves so as to form the letter H with their bodies

- Groups in which everyone shares a birth month or season

You can use this activity when you are preparing to form new cooperative groups or to get into preexisting ones. Simply end the exercise by describing the specific groups you wish to form. For example, you might tell students, "Get into groups with four others you have not yet worked with this year."

Another benefit of this activity is that within a class, grouping often causes distress for students. One of the most frightening commands for students can be "Find a partner." So much negative self-talk can go on when an instruction like this is given. Young people worry about not being liked, not being picked, what it all means personally and socially. When you give the students a set of instructions around which to form their groups, you move the focus from people and personalities to the descriptive details you have specified (Weinstein & Goodman, 1980).

Kitchen Capers

This is a timed, structured group experience that challenges students to practice the skills of negotiation, inclusion, compromise, and listening. Although this experience seems like a fun icebreaker, it is much more than that. This exercise has been known to cause some tense moments as time runs out and groups become increasingly stressed. As always, the critical aspect of this activity is in the processing.

Have students form groups of five to seven students. Give each group an envelope filled with the following materials:

- Two index cards
- Four toothpicks
- Two paper clips
- Two pencils
- One rubber band
- One balloon

Once the groups have the materials, give them 15 minutes to invent a kitchen item that "no kitchen should be without." The more creative the idea the better. All items in the envelopes must be used.

When the 15 minutes have elapsed, give teams 10 more minutes in which each must come up with a commercial to sell its product.

After a group has presented its commercial, process by asking some or all of the following questions:

- Did your invention change as you worked on it and if so, how?
- How did you come up with your final idea?
- Was everyone involved in some way?
- What roles did people play?
- Did you have a leader?
- Was a leader necessary? Why or why not?
- How did you feel when you completed your invention?
- How do you feel now?
- What would you like to say to your teammates?

GROUP-BUILDING EXERCISES

The range of exercises available for creating harmony and a sense of camaraderie within a classroom are infinite. You will be able to invent exercises that take off from the ones offered here. You may also wish to consult the Additional Resources in the Appendix (p. 119). I have included here a few of my favorite routines, which have also been favorites with my students. Some of the exercises foster listening and response skills, some teach how to join in a supportive environment, and a particularly useful set of exercises encourages team-building.

Listening and Response

Talking council: A variation on the class meeting. The *talking council* uses a *talking stick*. Students sit in a circle to talk about a specific issue. Only the person holding the stick may speak—the others listen. When a person is finished, that person turns to the person on the right, looks at that person and, while handing the stick over with both hands, addresses the person directly. "Jessie," a student might say, "how do you feel about this situation?" The stick keeps going around until everyone has finished. People may speak more than once if they have something else they would like to offer, but only when they are holding the stick. After all have finished, summarize to the class some of the key points made during the talking council.

The talking council highlights the importance of listening, of not interrupting, and of honoring others who are speaking. It also models how a group of individuals can talk about emotional issues in a caring, compassionate, and honorable way.

You can use any item as the talking stick (eraser, marker, feather, etc.), though the term becomes more meaningful if the class finds one large stick or other item from the school grounds. Each student can hang something of importance (a necklace, a picture, a stone) from the stick to personalize it for the group. One teacher I know had students make personal talking sticks out of paper. Each person decorated the paper with symbols or pictures of something important in his or her life, rolled the paper up, taped it, and used the roll as an individual talking stick.

Talking circle. The *talking circle* also uses a talking stick. The class forms two concentric circles. Those on the inside circle use the stick and speak to the issue presented (often a conflict involving only those who are speaking). Those in the outside circle listen and may take notes. After the inside circle has finished, the students on the outside circle provide summary statements reflecting *content* (what was said) and *process* (how things were said). Process statements are more challenging but they provide more insight into the dynamics of the issue and people who were speaking. A combination content/process statement would be: *I noticed that when the idea of fitting in came up and you talked about how hard it is to go against what the rest of the group is doing (content), Robert and Susan looked down and Diane and John took deep breaths (process).*

After one round, have people on the inside circle go to the outside and bring new people into the talking circle. The new people could offer additional observations about the situation, or they could provide suggestions for solutions to the conflict being discussed. After all people have had a turn to speak, form one large circle, summarize the theme of the talking circle (what the inner groups talked about), and run a class meeting to provide closure on the issues or topics that came up.

The Talking Circle is a variation of the process known as *Fishbowl* (Edwards, 1972), which is presented in much the same way, with the inner circle as the fish and outer circle as the bowl (because as the observers, those on the outside can see and hear what the "fish" are doing and saying).

Fact or fiction. In this storytelling game, students stand in a circle surrounding one who tells a story about his or her life.

The storyteller can tell tales about ancestors or about unusual life experiences. A storyteller may make up the story *(fiction)* or tell a true one *(fact)*. The storyteller is, however, trying to fool the audience. The strategy is to tell a true story that has a bit of the unbelievable or sensational in it, or to tell a made-up story that rings true for listeners.

After the telling, all listeners put their hands behind their backs, either crossing their index and middle fingers if they feel the story is fiction, or leaving those two fingers uncrossed if they feel the story is fact. Upon a prompt from you, all students show their crossed or uncrossed fingers, revealing their judgment of the story. The teller then confesses, saying whether the story was true to life or invented.

Students enjoy this game, and while they play they also are practicing the social skills of listening, speaking, decision making, and planning—while showing honor and respect to a peer. It feels good to share something about yourself with the group or to use your clever yarn-spinning ability to fool some classmates.

Joining a Supportive Environment

The give-away. The *give-away* is part of the Circle of Courage model of youth development created by Martin Brokenleg, Larry Brendtro, and Steve Van Bockern (2002). The Circle of Courage represents a synthesis of their research on tribal wisdom and is presented as a medicine wheel. The wheel is intended to illustrate the desire to create balance and harmony in a young person's life. Each direction on the wheel has a developmental need connected to it. In the East, the direction of sunrise, is the need for belonging and new beginnings. In the South, where the sun is highest in the noon sky, is mastery. In the West, where mystery and the setting sun reside, is independence. And in the North, where in the night sky wisdom reigns, generosity abounds.

The *give-away* is a process that works in the North, helping young people see and feel the joy and sense of significance and wisdom that come from Northern-direction practices. To give is to receive. This is a concept that, once understood, can be translated into generous acts.

Hold a talking council and ask the students to share their answers to the question "What is one of the nicest gifts you have ever received?" You will get a variety of answers covering both the material (*my bicycle, my stereo*) and the non-material (*my little sister, when my mom wasn't sick any more, my family, my life*). Process with the class about the many nonphysical gifts we receive and what they mean to us.

Brainstorm a *Priceless Gifts* list with your class, asking them to come up with ways to give someone a priceless gift—friendship, or a compliment, or a smile and hello. After the brainstorming, ask the class why the items on this list can be considered priceless.

Make the term "give-away" a part of your classroom language, connecting it with the idea of choosing to give something to another person. Discuss specific strategies for being caring, compassionate, friendly, and supportive as ways of being generous to others. Encourage students to practice the give-away on a regular basis, adding to the *Priceless Gifts* list every time they do so.

Some specific programmatic examples of a give-away approach are student mentoring and tutoring programs in which students who are trained in communication and empathy skills provide support and guidance either to younger students or to those peers who need academic or social support. In a program of this kind, everyone wins—both the person who is providing the generous act and the one who is the recipient.

I was involved for 6 years with a student mentoring program in the local junior and senior high schools (grades 7–12) in my community. The program paired a high school student with an incoming seventh grader who was in need of some extra support. Some of the relationships that evolved in the program continued for many years beyond high school. It was not unusual for former seventh-grade recipients to volunteer to become mentors when they got to high school, thereby creating a "give-*back.*"

Standing ovation. No one can get too much encouragement and positive feedback. And everyone loves a standing ovation. But standing ovations don't have to be reserved for what people do—they can be used to applaud who they are, too. You can provide students with the opportunity to give and receive standing ovations in your classroom. Here are the guidelines:

- Anyone can ask for a standing ovation at any time (except during a test).

- The person receiving the ovation has to raise both hands in the air in triumph, standing on a chair if so desired.

- If students request a "standing O" for a classmate, feeling that person could use some cheering up, the student must agree to it (students usually agree).

The power of standing ovations will bring a group closer together. The exercise is different, it is energizing, it demonstrates the joy of support, and it teaches how to ask for something you want (Weinstein & Goodman, 1980).

We missed you. There is a simple efficiency technique I like to use in the classroom whenever someone has been absent. It is a sheet of paper with "We missed you" printed at the top. Early in the year the students team up in pairs, and whenever a student is absent, his or her partner is responsible for recording each assignment or lesson covered during the school day. Arriving back in school, the student finds the "We missed you" sheet waiting on his or her desk. The partner then goes over the sheet with the returning student, offering further explanation if necessary. The first time I used this sheet, the student told me how nice it was that we missed her and that one of her classmates was looking out for her. What a wonderful lesson she taught me: To be missed and thought of is to feel important and a part of the group. The form we used looked like the one shown in Figure 3.1 on page 89.

Hidden talents. The purpose of this activity is to increase the students' awareness of themselves and others in the class, and to help them feel a stronger sense of connection to their classmates. Each student individually writes down one talent or skill he or she brings to the class. Students should think of something their classmates might not know about them. It is helpful to offer examples of things students might write. *I'm good at setting goals and reaching them*, for example, or *I listen well to others.* After students have written down talents, have them share using the following approach:

1. Seat the students in a circle (if possible).

Figure 3.1

We Missed You

For: _____ From: _____

Things we read today (with page numbers): _____
_____
_____
_____

Things we discussed today (summary):_____
_____
_____
_____

Things we did today (any special projects): _____
_____
_____
_____

Assignments:

1. _____

2. _____

3. _____

4. _____

5. _____

2. Before each person shares, others in the class guess aloud what they think that student wrote down as his or her talent.

3. After several guesses have been offered, the student reads what he or she actually wrote. Each turn is taken in this way.

4. After everyone has taken a turn, ask group members some or all of the following questions:

   • How do you feel right now (immediately after the exercise)?

   • How many of you have ever been told by your classmates what your talents are?

   • How did it feel to tell people what their talents were?

Close this exercise by describing the warm feeling people get when they hear something nice about themselves as "silent joy"—that feeling or sensation in your body when you feel relaxed, happy, and content. We can help people feel this silent joy by way of the things we say to them or do for them.

A variation on this process is to have each person in the group write a guess for the talent of another on an index card. When it is a person's turn to go, everyone displays the cards in front of them. The person whose turn it is can silently look around the circle, reading the feedback from the other students. At the end of the turn, that student gets to keep all of the cards.

Team-Building

Home team. To create a safe classroom setting where students will not be fearful of being hurt by others either verbally or physically, work with the class collaboratively to "name" a safe environment. You can do this with a simple brainstorming process.

Ask the class to brainstorm the answers to two questions:

1. What is it like to be on the visiting team?
2. What is it like to be on the home team?

Put the two lists side by side and compare them through a class dialogue. Ask which team people would rather be on. (Most will choose the home team because of the positive connotations.) As a class you can plan strategies to create a home-team environment in the classroom. For example,

- All students are made to feel comfortable.
- People cheer each other on.
- Students give each other standing ovations.
- People help each other if they're having a hard time.

The process here is key. This is not a situation in which the teacher dictates how people should act—this is a cooperative group process that invites input from all of the students.

Silent birthdays. This activity gets people moving around and communicating in a different way: without words. It is a non-threatening approach to beginning group-building. The group's task is to have everyone circle up in birthday order (date only, not year born). The goal is to end up with a circle starting with January and going month by month, ending with December with all students in the correct order. The hitch is that this must all be done silently: without words. This means that writing is not permitted either—not on paper, not on the ground, not in the air. People may communicate using only their fingers and a nod or shake of the head. The real learning from this activity comes from the processing when you, as teacher, ask: "What was it like to communicate without words?" The students will answer either that it was fun or that it was hard and frustrating. If they give the second answer, ask them what was hard about it. This should provide an opportunity for a class meeting in which to explore further the difficulties that can arise when people do not understand each other, and how important it is to be patient when working with people who do not see things the way you do.

Boundary-breaking. This team-building experience facilitates the practice of openness within small groups of students. You can change the questions to accommodate the age group with which you are working.

1. Seat the group in a circle.

2. Have each person answer each question (explain that people may pass if necessary and you will come back to them).

3. The leader should repeat the answer of each person if necessary (some people do not speak loudly in this setting). Positive encouragement is essential. Keep all students comfortable and informed.

4. Group members may not repeat someone else's answer.

5. Questions are not to be explained or limited. Each person is to react to what he or she hears. Keep the mood serious at all times. If a person does not understand a question, repeat it with the same wording.

When you set up this exercise, you may offer students directions like these: *We are going to respond to a series of questions. Every answer you give is absolutely right. No one will question it. Simply respond to what you hear. We will proceed around the circle, starting with a different person each time. If you can't think of an answer when it's your turn, say "pass" and I'll come back to you later. Please don't let me forget you. We are here to practice our listening skills and to be supportive of each person in this group. We are to honor each person's answers so that we may learn more about our classmates.*

Questions you may wish to use include these:

- What time of day do you like best and for what reason?
- What is your favorite season?
- What is your favorite television show?
- What is the nicest gift you ever received?
- What is the happiest day you can remember?
- What do you do best?
- What is your greatest fear?
- How do you feel when people judge you?
- What do you look for in a friend?
- How would you describe people in your age group?
- How would your parent or guardian describe you?
- What would you like to be doing 10 years from now?
- What do you need most from others?
- What can you give others?

When you and the students have finished with the first question set, you may move on to the *Synthesis Set.*

Tell students: *Answer these questions based on what you just heard your classmates say.*

- What was the hardest question to answer and for what reason?
- Who did you learn the most about?
- Who are you most curious about?
- Whose answers surprised you?
- Who do you feel closer to now?

Human treasure hunt. This activity helps people mix with one another, learn about each other, make connections, be actively involved, and practice their listening skills. Activities like this one are informal group builders. Students are encouraged to gather new information about their classmates in a less structured way.

Give students copies of a form like the one shown in Figure 3.2 on page 95. Give them these instructions:

Walk around the group, finding people who fit the statements listed on the form. Ask questions. (Do you like to listen to others?) Have any person who responds positively write his or her name by the statement that applies to him or her. Be sure to ask a follow-up question. (What is the reason you like to listen to others?) Write that additional information in the space provided.

Closure

Closure is a term used to describe the healthy conclusion to an activity. It is used in particular to refer to an ending in which

Figure 3.2

Human Treasure Hunt

Name _____

_____ 1. Likes to listen to others _____

_____

_____ 2. Avoids confrontation _____

_____

_____ 3. Tries new things_____

_____

_____ 4. Plans ahead _____

_____

_____ 5. Gets along with lots of people _____

_____

_____ 6. Has a dream about the future_____

_____

_____ 7. Cares about his or her classmates _____

_____

_____ 8. Feels misunderstood sometimes_____

_____

_____ 9. Likes to help people _____

_____

_____10. Belongs to a club or school organization _____

_____

a group identifies what has been learned and comes away from an experience with a sense of satisfaction. Closure can describe the ending of a school year when the class experience comes to an end, or it can refer to the ending of an activity or lesson. People in groups need a sense of coming to the end of an activity. Formal closure helps people focus as they move on to the next part of their day with others—they are not distracted by looking back. The following exercises are helpful in delineating activities for students and letting them see what they have learned.

Honorable endings. As a group gets ready to adjourn or when an activity is about to end, it is important to provide a forum to take care of any unfinished business. This exercise helps people establish connections within the group one final time. It is done in a class-meeting format in which some or all of the following questions (whichever ones you feel are necessary) are asked, one at a time, in a "whip-a-round" (around the circle) form of sharing.

- What expressions of gratitude would you like to share?
- What touched you during the experience (an expression of feelings)?
- How/when were you challenged?
- Is there any apology or explanation that needs to be offered to anyone in the group?
- Who surprised you in the group?
- Who are you more curious about now?
- Who did you learn the most about?

- Is there one thing you can say you have learned from this experience?

- Is there anything else you would like to say at this time?

Just before the last question, a colleague of mine would say, "if anyone has been rehearsing something to say this is your last chance to say it." This would often elicit laughter and encourage some hesitant people who really wanted to speak. It provided them with just the push they needed to share their thoughts or feelings.

Sentence stems. A *sentence stem* is an incomplete sentence left for the students to finish. It is an efficient and effective vehicle for coming to closure. The following sentence stems are useful in a classroom setting:

> *One thing I learned is . . .*
> *Right now I feel . . .*
> *I wish . . .*
> *One thing that surprised me is . . .*
> *I hope . . .*
> *One way we can improve is . . .*

If someone's sentence stem is different in feeling and tone from the others (everyone is enthusiastic and delighted, say, except one person), wait until all have gone and ask for clarification. This is not to challenge the person or put him or her on the spot, but to give that person a chance to express needs, and thus to validate them.

Gift of happiness. I have used this activity at the close of a group experience. Each student receives a legal-size envelope and a piece of masking tape. Students write their names on the backs of the envelopes and decorate them any way they wish.

Students are to write positive messages to all the members in their group expressing a specific appreciation to each person. An example of a positive message is this:

Dear Jerry: Thank you for being patient with me when I didn't understand what my responsibility was. You explained it to me and I was able to complete my task. Your friend, Jim.

When all have finished writing their messages, they wait to deliver them until instructed to do so. Students tape their envelopes to their backs with the name showing outward. After all have finished writing messages to each student in their group and all have taped envelopes to their backs, students walk around the room depositing the messages in the envelopes taped to others' backs.

When all have received their messages, allow them to read their messages, then let them process the experience in a community meeting (see page 59). After the meeting, students seal their envelopes and take them home. You can use the Gift of Happiness exercise at various junctures during the school year.

What have you learned? This is an exercise that can be helpful almost anytime. It is a wonderful way to help students focus on the progress of their learning. It's also very simple: Throughout a lesson or learning experience ask the students, "What have you learned so far?" It is an important question because articulating what you have learned can help others identify what *they* have learned. By encouraging this kind of reflection throughout the lesson and not just at the end, you are keeping students engaged and focused.

Section Four

Teaching Empathy

From empathy to compassion is but a step.

—Frederick Franck, *Fingers Pointing Toward the Sacred*

WITH ALL THE COMMUNITY-BUILDING EXERCISES detailed in the previous section and all the discussion of cultures of caring and the skills of listening, sharing, honoring, and respecting, we have been approaching the sentiment upon which all healthy social interaction is dependent: empathy.

I would have simply left the exercises as they were and not added this separate section devoted to the fostering of empathy, had it not been for an experience I had while teaching a particular class.

THE BIRTH OF A PROCESS

One cold winter day in a workshop for eighth-grade students in upstate New York, when we were discussing the courage it takes to stand up for another person, we spontaneously created a three-step process that led toward an empathic action. I starting making up a series of challenging scenarios about others, about the experiences these hypothetical others might be going through, and together we came up with three questions: *What happened to the person? How is that person feeling?* and *What could be done to help and support the person?* We went through this series of questions a few times, realizing their extraordinary effectiveness, and thus the Event Empathy Action method (EEA) was born.

Since that day, I have taught EEA to hundreds of students in social-skills and anti-bullying learning sessions. It is the impact of these sessions that has inspired me to include EEA in this book. It is my hope that the Event Empathy Action method will help play a role in creating a safe, compassionate, supportive, and nurturing community experience for all students.

EMPATHY

Empathy is the ability to vicariously feel what another person is feeling, to understand and connect to where that person is. This is a high level of human insight, for it is an "awareness that makes it possible to identify with the life process in other living beings" (MacIver, 1999, p. 17). It is a loosening of personal limits, as Naperstek (1997) points out. "When our boundaries open to include others and we allow ourselves to feel what they feel and see what they see, the natural end result is a kinder, more caring behavior" (p. 175). Empathy is a social skill, and as such it can be taught, practiced, and applied. It is positively associated with a broad range of other prosocial behaviors such as cooperation, sociability, and interpersonal competence, and is negatively associated with aggressive behavior (Goldstein, 1999). The experiences we as educators provide for young people in inculcating empathy and other prosocial behaviors can have a profound impact on their emotional lives as well as on the lives of others.

DEFINING EEA

Event Empathy Action (EEA) is a three-step advanced listening approach that teaches students how to respond to others empathically. When something unfortunate, disappointing, or sad (a family separation, doing poorly on a test, not being invited to a party, being embarrassed in front of others) happens in another person's life, the following open-ended questions are asked internally. Initially students are led through these questions by the teacher. The hope is that in time they will naturally (or automatically) respond to others by thinking through these three questions:

- What happened? *(the event)*
- How is that person feeling? *(empathy)*
- What will I do? *(a specific action)*

The EEA method is presented to the group using *empathic situations*—hypothetical scenarios a class can discuss in order to explore various empathic responses.

PRESENTING EEA

Have a class meeting (see page 59) and, using a story, song, poem, video, or other teaching tool (see Additional Resources section, page 119), focus on the concept of empathy. Students often know what *sympathy* means, and can successfully define it in terms of feeling sorry for another. You can explain that *empathy* is similar but does not mean exactly the same thing. Empathy is not about pity, but about an act of imagination, about being able, as the saying goes, to walk a mile in someone else's shoes.

Read the script of an empathic situation to the group. Such a script will depict a specific situation in which a decision about behavior toward another has to be made. The dilemma lies in the question "What is the empathy action?" After reading the situation script, ask the sequence of questions presented in the EEA Method (the three steps) by inscribing the students' answers in three frames.

Here is an example of an empathic situation script to use in teaching EEA. You will explain the hypothetical situation to the class, then engage in the dialogue prescribed in the script.

Situation (read by teacher): There's a new student in school who is sitting alone at recess.

Instructions (read by teacher): Let's look at how you would respond if you were the student. Together, let's go through the EEA method by answering the requisite series of three questions.

Teacher: Tell us what's going on. (event)

Student: The new kid is sitting alone.

Teacher: How is the new student feeling? (empathy)

Student: Alone and maybe mad or afraid.

Teacher: So what specific action would you take? (action)

Student: I would go up to him, introduce myself, and ask if I could sit with him.

At this point, review EEA using a wall chart that has the three steps identified, clarify if necessary, and read a second empathic situation following the same group dialogue approach.

Empathic situations. The following situations are for use in practicing EEA. As in the above example, you read a situation to the class, then facilitate a dialogue using the three EEA questions in which various empathic responses are explored. It is important to point out to your students that often the best thing to do for others is to give them space. Leaving others alone but letting them know you are there if they need you is a choice in and of itself. Other times, the action involves doing something specific, such as helping a person pick up his books and asking if he's okay. The practice of empathy and support is an inexact science, but if the compassionate intent is constant, the automatic response will reflect this as students do the best they can.

- Joanne had mud splashed onto her clothes at the bus stop and two other girls laughed at her. Joanne tried to hide her tears but it was obvious she was crying.

- Your friend Philip did poorly on his math test and you did well. After the teacher handed the tests back, Philip took one look at his grade and froze. Everyone was supposed to be correcting their tests, but Philip wasn't moving. He was just staring down at his paper.

- During lunch Jamal accidentally dropped his tray on the floor. Everyone started applauding and laughing.

- Mira is a new girl in school. On her first day, you ate lunch with her and the two of you hung together at recess. Kamala (your closest friend) didn't want to hang out with the new girl and got mad at you. When you asked her what was wrong she said "we're not best friends anymore."

- During gym class, Lupe fell, hurt her knee, and had to go to the nurse's office. When she came back to class, you could tell she had been crying.

- Your closest friend's mom just had a baby.

- Most of the kids in your class, including you, were invited to a party. Randy was not invited. Even though he says he doesn't care, you think he might be upset.

- Rachel forgot her homework and was upset when she arrived at school.

- Your brother just got a great report card.

- During a soccer game, one of your teammates kicked the ball into the wrong goal. Everyone yelled at her and she started crying.

As a class, create your own empathic situations to consider. Or, as the teacher or group leader, you can make them up from real situations you've seen young people experience.

EEA Rotation

Have students circle up in groups of three. Provide the students with hypothetical events in which EEA can be practiced. Have each person in the group do a step in the process. The first person describes what happened (**event**), the second explains how the person involved might be feeling (**empathy**), and the third proposes the specific response to make (**action**). When they have finished, offer another situation and have the students trade roles. Each group goes through three situations so that every student gets an opportunity to practice each role.

Role-Plays

Have students individually write about situations they have experienced in which they needed someone to respond empathically. Put the students in pairs. Have partners ask, *What happened?* and *How did you feel?* about the identified situation. Then have the questioner offer an empathic reflection, i.e., *You must have been feeling really frustrated.*

Pairs share their dialogue by role-playing in front of the class. The teacher or facilitator processes by asking the role-players clarifying questions about the situation.

Sample role-play

Student 1: What happened?

Student 2: I wasn't paying attention when we switched goals in the soccer game and I kicked the ball into the wrong goal. Then everyone started yelling at me.

Student 1: How did you feel?

Student 2: Embarrassed and angry.

Student 1: (Offering an empathic reflection) You must have been really upset. They shouldn't have yelled at you. That could happen to anyone.

After each role-play, thank the students who shared and ask the class to identify the empathy action. Students may offer other empathy action suggestions.

Role-playing is an effective approach for helping students internalize a new concept. Edward Moody, speaking at the Morals in Education Conference in April 1999, warned that it is important to the success of the exercise that the following conditions exist:

- The role-play should be in continuity with the lesson.

- The guidance or instructions must be clear.

- The students must be challenged by the role-play and feel the support of the teacher and classmates.

- There should be a combination of *experience* and *reflection,* either through class dialogue, journal writing, or some other approach.

EEA Journaling

Journaling provides students with the opportunity for self-reflection. In EEA journaling the student describes in journal format the situation that requires an empathy action. The purpose of EEA journaling is to allow students another avenue for imaginative access to empathic emotions. Writing allows students to put themselves in the moment, so that more thoughts, feelings, and ideas emerge. It also increases the likelihood of internalizing EEA responses.

A student doing EEA journaling might write something like this: *One day during recess, this new kid was sitting all by himself. He was looking down. He must have been feeling very alone and scared. I went over to him, introduced myself, and asked him to join us in the game we were playing.*

Have students share their journal entries with partners, dialoguing about the situation and the action that was or might have been taken. Figure 4.1 on page 107 shows a sample Journal Entry Form.

Declarations

After completing a series of lessons on empathy, have each student write down one specific and realistic empathic declaration that can be acted upon within one week. A student might

---

Figure 4.1

EEA Journal Entry Form

Name_____

Write your empathy action as a journal entry. You may use either real-life situations or situations you imagine for this purpose.

1. Write an entry that includes contemplation of the following questions:

   a. What happened and to whom? (event)

   b. How did that person feel? (empathy)

   c. What would you do for that person? (action)

Sample: *Gene felt embarrassed because everyone laughed at him when he got the wrong answer. I wanted to help Gene feel better so I told him that he'll have another chance and it will be okay.*

2. Write what you have learned (or imagine you might learn, if you're making up the event).

Sample: *I learned that if you encourage someone, it might help cheer them up.*

---

write, for example, *I will help someone who doesn't understand the assignment in Language Arts*, or *I will say hello to three younger students this week.* Have students share their declarations in pairs, reminding them to be listeners for each other. Then, in a class meeting, have each student stand up and declare the specific caring or empathic action he or she plans to take. The sequence of writing, sharing in pairs, and verbalizing the declaration in front of others increases the chances for follow-through because it brings the declaration to life.

Rapid EEA Practice: Empathy → Action

The ultimate goal of this training is to help students to internalize EEA as an automatic two-step process: Empathy → Action. The way to facilitate this automatic response is to have Empathy → Action sessions during a class meeting in which a situation is recounted and students are asked to immediately identify the Empathy → Action (see Figure 4.2 on page 109).

HOW TO TEACH THE EEA APPROACH

When you set out to teach EEA, it may be helpful to have a map of where you are headed. The following list may clarify for you the sequence of steps I recommend for this approach.

1. Lesson on understanding differences between people and the need to belong (You might want to use the "Howard Gray" video. See the Additional Resources section.)

2. What is listening? (See pages 53–56)

3. Listening practice in pairs (See suggested exercise, page 57)

4. Community meeting: dialogue on caring (See community meeting suggestions, page 59)

5. EEA introduced and practiced (pp. 100–104)

6. Practice using group dialogue, EEA rotation, and role plays (pp. 104–106)

7. EEA journaling (p. 106)

Figure 4.2

Rapid Practice Empathy → Action Scenario

Work with pairs of students who have shown facility in internalizing the three-step process. Allow the rest of the class to participate by shouting out suggestions when needed.

Teacher: *Your sister wasn't invited to a party. What's she feeling?*

Student 1: *She feels left out and hurt.*

Teacher: *What's your action?*

Student 1: *I would listen to her and let her know I am there for her.*

Student 2: *How about taking her to a movie to let her know you care and maybe to take her mind off it?*

When learning a new social skill, especially one as complex as empathy, students benefit from multiple practice sessions. Rapid practice can be done efficiently as a rehearsal for real-life situations.

---

8. Empathic declarations (pp. 106–108)

9. Periodic rapid empathy → action practice (p. 108)

ASSESSING THE NEED FOR EEA

The following two assessment tools are useful for focusing attention on the need for EEA training. The first assessment (Figure 4.3) can be used in talking to colleagues about the importance of empathy training. The second assessment (Figure 4.4) focuses on individual students and is useful in the classroom.

Figure 4.3

Empathy Education Needs Assessment

When considering the need for EEA training in your school, ask the following questions:

1. Is listening taught and practiced school-wide (by staff, students, and parents)?   ___yes ___no

2. Does the staff understand that the three low-level forms of aggressive behavior are teasing, harassment, and put-downs?   ___yes ___no

3. Are teasing, bullying, and other aggressive behaviors prohibited?   ___yes ___no

4. Are students taught to recognize and admire empathetic behavior?   ___yes ___no

5. Is staff behavior empathetic and are connections made with all students?   ___yes ___no

6. Is staff trained in social skills development?

                    ___yes ___no

7. Is the teaching of empathy and other social skills integrated into the school's program and activities?   ___yes ___no

8. Are parents offered workshops on the importance of empathy and other social skills?   ___yes ___no

If the answers to more than two of these questions are No, your school may be due for some EEA training.

The following Student Empathy Assessment sheet is useful for getting students to think about empathy as a learnable skill. It's a good tool for focusing student minds before teaching EEA.

The teacher can use the completed assessments to determine which aspects of empathy or social skills are most important to teach the class. Or, the teacher may conference with each student to facilitate a dialogue to collectively decide on which aspect of empathy the student would like to work on. This could be done before teaching the EEA unit. The questions in the assessment are based on those used in the Skillstreaming Checklist from *The Prepare Curriculum*, by Goldstein, 1999 (pp.110–113).

Figure 4.4

Student Empathy Assessment

Name:_____ Date:_____

An assessment measures how well you do something. Just as a thermometer measures temperature, this assessment measures empathy. Empathy means being able to understand what another person is feeling. You will know if you are practicing empathy when you act in certain ways—like telling someone they played a good game. As you go through this assessment, think about the time you have spent with others in and out of school and rate how well you have practiced empathy.

    Circle 1 if you almost never use the skill.
    Circle 2 if you seldom use the skill.
    Circle 3 if you sometimes use the skill.
    Circle 4 if you often use the skill.
    Circle 5 if you almost always use the skill.

(continued)

Figure 4.4 (continued)

1. I listen when someone is talking to me.

   1   2   3   4   5

2. I ask open-ended questions when I need or want to know more.

   1   2   3   4   5

3. I summarize what I hear when someone is telling me something.

   1   2   3   4   5

4. I understand how other people are feeling.

   1   2   3   4   5

5. I help other people who need or want help.

   1   2   3   4   5

6. I say nice things to others after a game about how they played.

   1   2   3   4   5

7. I let people know when I feel a friend has not been treated fairly.

   1   2   3   4   5

8. I offer to share what I have with others.

   1   2   3   4   5

9. I let others know when I care about them.

   1   2   3   4   5

10. I recognize when others do something they feel proud of.

    1   2   3   4   5

Epilogue

Our Collective Purpose

SINCE I BEGAN WRITING THIS BOOK a great deal has happened in the world. I ask this question: How can we nurture a sense of hope, optimism, safety, and trust—the cornerstones of community—for our students in a world that at times seems so hopeless, negative, unsafe, and uncertain? The challenge for educators, more than ever, is to create conditions of emotional safety while inviting our students to imagine what life can offer them and what they can offer life.

We must take the immense responsibility of this moment and see ourselves as teachers stirring the alchemical brew, bringing together the hearts and souls of children as they grow toward adulthood. Your classroom community can be a place where students love to learn and share in the learning process with others. The classroom community is really all about the creation of caring relationships; how people relate to the world, each other, and themselves.

As you continue to build community, allow the process to bring you to a place of inner-growth and joy—the same place to which you have brought your students. A fitting conclusion to this book is the story of Mrs. Wist—a true solution-maker who built classroom communities with her own special brand of caring.

Eleanor Wist taught kindergarten from 1970–1990 in Pittsburgh, Pennsylvania. In the early years of her teaching career when her classes were smaller, Mrs. Wist visited the homes of her students before the school year started. She wanted to meet the children and their parents, hoping to make them feel more comfortable.

As her classes grew in size, Mrs. Wist began sending invitations to her students before school began, inviting them to come in and pick out their seats. When they arrived, Mrs. Wist introduced herself and welcomed them into the classroom.

Each week, Mrs. Wist and her husband invited four different children to their home for dinner. This continued until all kindergartners had been to dinner at the Wists' home. "I wanted to get to know them in a different setting," Mrs. Wist explains. "They would come in the next day talking about what they did."

During dinner each child had a job. After dinner Mrs. Wist's husband took the children into his workshop, where he showed them his tools and gave each a polished stone. They then played a game before Mr. Wist drove them home in his diesel truck. "They loved getting a ride in that truck," Mrs. Wist says.

Mrs. Wist kept track of what was happening with her former students through the local newspapers. When her first class was preparing to graduate from high school, she looked up each student in the high school yearbook. She then wrote each student a personal note, tucked it into a graduation card, and sent it to his or her home. Mrs. Wist continued this practice even after she retired.

The class of 2002 was Mrs. Wist's final class of former students. Following are excerpts from some of the letters this 83-year-old retired teacher has received:

> *I thank you from the bottom of my heart. I don't think I would have done as well without the wonderful start you gave me.*

> *The experiences I received in your classroom proved to be the foundation for my future learning. I still identify eating dinner at your house as one of my fondest childhood memories.*

> *Thank you so much for your card. . . . You will be in my thoughts as I become a teacher.*

Appendix

FIFTY SOCIAL SKILLS TO CONSIDER

If you have an interest in identifying your students' needs and competencies, the following exhaustive list of social skills, identified by Goldstein in his book *The Prepare Curriculum* (1999, pp. 114–119), may be helpful. I offer this list as a starting point for those working toward building classroom communities through the essential work of developing group and social skills among students.

Group I: Beginning Social Skills

- Listening
- Saying thank you
- Starting a conversation
- Having a conversation
- Introducing yourself
- Introducing other people
- Asking a question
- Giving a compliment

Group II: Advanced Social Skills

- Asking for help
- Joining in
- Giving instructions
- Following instructions
- Apologizing
- Convincing others

Group III. Skills for Dealing With Feelings

- Knowing your feelings
- Expressing your feelings

- Understanding the feelings of others
- Expressing affection
- Rewarding yourself
- Dealing with someone else's anger
- Dealing with fear

Group IV. Skills Alternatives to Aggression

- Asking permission
- Helping others
- Using self-control
- Responding to teasing
- Keeping out of fights
- Sharing something
- Negotiating
- Standing up for your rights
- Avoiding trouble with others

Group V: Skills for Dealing With Stress

- Making a complaint
- Being a good sport
- Standing up for a friend
- Responding to failure
- Dealing with an accusation
- Getting ready for a difficult conversation
- Answering a complaint
- Dealing with embarrassment
- Dealing with being left out
- Responding to persuasion
- Dealing with contradictory messages
- Dealing with group pressure

Group VI: Planning Skills

- Deciding on something to do
- Setting a goal
- Gathering information
- Making a decision
- Deciding what caused a problem
- Deciding on your abilities
- Arranging problems by importance
- Concentrating on a task

SOCIAL SKILLS AUDIT

The purpose of this audit is for a teacher to determine in which social skills students do not demonstrate competency. In order to build a unified classroom community where students get along, work together, and have the capacity to overcome conflicts, it is imperative that students demonstrate specific social competencies.

1. Write down your observations of your students' behaviors in the space below:

   _____
   _____
   _____
   _____
   _____
   _____
   _____
   _____
   _____

2. Are students lacking in skills in any of the following areas?
   • Beginning social skills (greeting, manners, having a conversation)
   • Advanced social skills (expressing what they need)
   • Dealing with feelings
   • Alternatives to aggression
   • Dealing with stress
   • Planning

3. Choose a skill from the above list and develop a lesson using the following social skills template.

Social Skills Teaching Template

1. Skill: _____

2. Reason for choosing this skill: _____
   _____
   _____
   _____

3. Introducing the skill: What is your framing statement?_____
   _____
   _____
   _____

4. Modeling the skill: How will you model the skill for your class?
   _____
   _____
   _____

5. Present the guidelines for the skill and identify what they are.

6. Assign students to work in pairs to practice the skill.
   Process with the class: What questions will you ask? _____
   _____
   _____
   _____

7. Homework: Will you assign students to practice the skill at
   home? _____
   _____
   _____
   _____

ADDITIONAL RESOURCES

Peer Leadership, A Human Relations Process to Reduce Substance Abuse and Improve School Climate, by Thomas Turney. (1994). Mountainside, NJ: Turney.

Playfair, Everybody's Guide to Noncompetitive Play, by Matt Weinstein and Joel Goodman. (1980). San Luis Obispo, CA: Impact.

Second Step: A Violence Prevention Curriculum (grades K–9). (2002). Seattle, WA: The Committee for Children.

The Hundred Dresses, by Eleanor Estes. (1973). New York: Scholastic.

The Morning Meeting Book, by Roxann Kriete. (2001). Greenfield, MA: The Northeast Foundation for Children.

The Peer Partners Handbook: Helping Your Friends Live Free From Violence, Drug Use, Teen Pregnancy & Suicide, by Jerry Kreitzer and David A. Levine. (1995). Barrytown, NY: Station Hill Press.

The Prepare Curriculum: Teaching Prosocial Competencies, by Arnold P. Goldstein. (1999). Champaign, IL: Research Press.

The Teacher's Vocation: Nurturing the Imagination of Others. (2001). A talk by poet David Whyte on CD or cassette. Langley, WA: Many Rivers.

This Same Sky: A Collection of Poems From Around the World, selected by Naomi Shihab Nye. (1992). New York: Four Winds Press, Macmillan.

Through the Eyes of Howard Gray, by David A. Levine. (1996). Accord, NY: Blue Heron Press.

Set Straight on Bullies, by John Hoover and the National Safety Center. (1988). Bloomington, IN: Solution Tree (formerly National Educational Service).

TRAINING RESOURCES

Animas Valley Institute: www.animas.org

Committee for Children: www.cfchildren.org

Developmental Studies Center: www.devstu.org

Developmental Therapy-Teaching Programs: www.uga.edu/dttp

Educators for Social Responsibility: www.esrnational.org

In Care of Students: www.incareofstudents.org

Northeast Foundation for Children: www.responsiveclassroom.org

Reclaiming Youth International: www.reclaiming.com

Search Institute: www.search-institute.org

Solution Tree: www.solution-tree.com

References

Arrien, A. (1993). *The four-fold way: Walking the paths of the warrior, teacher, healer and visionary.* San Francisco: HarperCollins.

Benard, B. (1991). *Fostering resiliency in kids: Protective factors in family, school, and community.* San Francisco: Far West Laboratory for Educational Research and Development and the Western Regional Center for Drug Free Schools and Communities.

Bogenschneider, K., Small, S., & Riley, D. (1991). National Extension Youth at Risk. *An ecological, risk-focused approach for addressing youth at-risk issues.* Chevy Chase, MD: National 4-H Center, Wisconsin Extension.

Brendtro, L., Brokenleg, M., & Van Bockern, S. (2002). *Reclaiming youth at risk: Our hope for the future.* Bloomington, IN: Solution Tree (formerly National Educational Service).

Brown, M. Y. (1983). *The unfolding self: Psychosynthesis and counseling.* Los Angeles: Psychosynthesis Press.

Cooper, R. K., & Sawaf, A. (1997). *Executive EQ: Emotional intelligence in leadership and organizations.* New York: Berkley.

Costa, A. L., & Kallick, B. (2000). *Discovering and exploring habits of mind: Book 1.* Alexandria, VA: Association for Supervision and Curriculum Development.

Durant, W. (1953). *The story of civilization: Part V, the Renaissance.* New York: Simon & Schuster.

Edwards, G. (1972). *Reaching out: The prevention of drug abuse through increased human interaction.* Barrytown, NY: Station Hill Press.

Edwards, G. (1990). *Impact teaching.* Sayville, NY: Impact Strategists.

Franck, F. (1994). *Fingers pointing toward the sacred: A twentieth century pilgrimage on the eastern and western way.* Junction City, OR: Beacon Point Press.

Freire, P. (1990). *Pedagogy of the Oppressed.* New York: Continuum.

Fulghum, R. (1988). *All I really need to know I learned in kindergarten: Uncommon thoughts on common things.* New York: Villard Books.

Glasser, W. (1990). *The quality school: Managing students without coercion.* New York: Harper Perennial.

Glenn, H. S., & Nelson, J. (1989). *Raising self-reliant children in a self-indulgent world.* Rocklin, CA: Prima.

Goldstein, A. P., (1999). *The prepare curriculum: Teaching prosocial comptencies.* Champaign, IL: Research Press.

Goleman, D. (1998). *Working with emotional intelligence.* New York: Bantam Press.

Greenleaf, R. K. (1991). *Creating mind sets: Movies of the mind.* Naragansett, RI: Greenleaf Learning.

Hawkins, D., & Catalano, R. (1992). *Communities that care: Action for drug abuse prevention.* San Francisco: JosseyBass.

Holder, J. (1999). *Adventurelore: Adventure-based counseling for individuals and groups.* Holmes Beach, FL: Learning Publications Inc.

Hoover, J. H., & Oliver, R. (1996). *The bullying prevention handbook: A guide for principals, teachers, and counselors.* Bloomington, IN: Solution Tree (formerly National Educational Service).

Hoover, J. H., & Olsen, G. W. (2001). *Teasing and harassment: The frames and scripts approach for teachers and parents.* Bloomington, IN: Solution Tree (formerly National Educational Service).

Kohn, A. (1996). *Beyond discipline: From compliance to community.* Alexandria, VA: Association for Supervision and Curriculum Development.

Lew, J. (December, 1985). Workshop on Shaping Behavior for the Adelphi Univeristy National Training Institute. Week-long alcohol and other drug prevention training program.

Maslow, A. H., (1993). *The farther reaches of human nature.* New York: Penguin.

Naperstek, B. (1997). *Your sixth sense: Activating your psychic potential.* San Francisco: HarperCollins.

Osbon, D. K. (1991). *Reflections on the art of living: A Joseph Campbell companion.* New York: HarperCollins.

Remen, R. N. (1996). *Kitchen table wisdom: Stories that heal.* New York: Riverhead Books.

Rogers, C. (1980). *A way of being.* Boston: Houghton Mifflin.

Schimmoeller, C. (1999). In *A dance with the woods. Heron Dance,* 20, 17. MacIver, R. (ed.)

Schrumpf, F., Crawford, D., & Chu, U. H. (1991). *Peer mediation: Conflict resolution in schools.* Champaign, IL: Research Press.

Senge P., Roberts, C., & Ross, R. (1994). *The fifth discipline fieldbook: Strategies and tools for building a learning organization.* New York: Doubleday.

Some, M. (1996). *Ritual, the Sacred and Community* in *Crossroads: The quest for contemporary rites of passage.* Mahdi, L.C., Christopher, N.G. & Meade, M. (eds.). Chicago: Open Court.

Stein, H.T., & Edwards, M.E. (1998). Classical Adlerian Theory and Practice. In P. Marcus & A. Rosenberg (Eds.) *Psychoanalytic Versions of the Human Condition: Philosophies of Life and Their Impact on Practice.* New York: New York University Press.

Tafoya, T., (June 1992). Keynote address North Carolina Healthful Living Institute.

Turney, T. (1994). *Peer leadership: A human relations process to reduce substance abuse and improve school climate.* Mountainside, NJ: Turney.

Weinstein, M., & Goodman, J. (1980). *Playfair: Everyone's guide to noncompetitive play.* San Luis Obispo, CA: Impact.

Werner, E. E. (April 1989). Children of the garden island. *Scientific American, 260*(4), 106–111.

Werner, E. E., & Smith, R. S. (1992). *Overcoming the odds: High risk children from birth to adulthood.* Ithaca, NY: Cornell University Press.

Whyte, D. (1997). *The house of belonging.* Langley, WA: Many Rivers Press.

Zukav, G. (1990). *The seat of the soul.* New York: Simon & Schuster.

About the Author

DAVID A. LEVINE is a teacher, author, facilitator, and musician who has been working with students, teachers, and parents across the United States and abroad since 1984. He is the founder and director of In Care of Students—a training, development, and research group devoted to creating "Schools of Belonging." The emphasis is on musical expression, social skills development, leadership training, community-building initiatives, and curriculum design and implementation.

Levine was previously the chief trainer for the Northeast Regional Center's Safe and Drug Free Schools Program for the U.S. Department of Education, an elementary and middle school teacher, and has offered training sessions, workshops, and keynote speeches for hundreds of school districts, state agencies, and other educational organizations across the country. Since returning from a vision quest in the canyons of the Utah desert in October 1998, Levine has sought to incorporate much of what he discovered from that sacred experience into his interactions with young people and the adults who work with them.

David A. Levine is the author or co-author of several books, including *The Peer Partners Handbook* and *Teaching Empathy*. His educational programs and recordings include the bullying-prevention music video program *Through the Eyes of Howard*

Gray, which has been used by hundreds of school districts and numerous state departments of education, and *Dance of a Child's Dreams,* a recipient of the Parent's Choice Gold Award for children's music. His articles have appeared in the journals *Educational Leadership, Reclaiming Children and Youth,* and *School Safety.* He lives with his family in New York's Hudson River Valley.

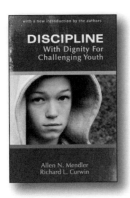

Discipline With Dignity For Challenging Youth
Allen N. Mendler and Richard L. Curwin
Create positive change in your most challenging students with the help of proven, practical strategies found in this resource. **BKF229**

Adventure Education for the Classroom Community
Laurie S. Frank and Ambrose Panico
New edition! Engaging activities encourage your students to create a classroom community that supports character development, academic excellence, and individual and social responsibility.
BKF221

The Bullying Prevention Handbook: A Guide for Principals, Teachers, and Counselors
John H. Hoover and Ronald L. Oliver
Second Edition! Solve bully-victim problems through education, mediation, and cultivation of respect and caring. New chapters explore modern-day issues like cyberbullying, "gay bashing," and more.
BKF233

Motivating Students Who Don't Care: Successful Techniques for Educators
Allen N. Mendler
Proven strategies and five effective processes empower you to reawaken motivation in students who aren't prepared, don't care, and won't work. **BKF102**